A Journey into Mohawk and Oneida Country, 1634–1635

The Iroquois and Their Neighbors

Christopher Vecsey, *Series Editor*

1. *Fort Orange, Rensselaerswijck (Albany, New York), circa 1650.*
Painting by L. F. Tantillo. © 2009 by Leonard F. Tantillo. Used
by permission of Leonard F. Tantillo.

A Journey into Mohawk and Oneida Country, 1634–1635

The Journal of Harmen Meyndertsz van den Bogaert

REVISED EDITION

Translated and edited by
CHARLES T. GEHRING
and
WILLIAM A. STARNA

Wordlist and linguistic notes by
GUNTHER MICHELSON

SYRACUSE UNIVERSITY PRESS

First Paperback Edition 1991
First Revised Edition 2013

20 21 22 23 34 25   7 6 5 4 3 2

∞ The paper used in this publication meets the minimum require-
ments of the American National Standard for Information Sciences—
Permanence of Paper for Printed Library Materials, ANSI Z39.48-
1992.

For a listing of books published and distributed by Syracuse University
Press, visit https://press.syr.edu.

ISBN: 978-0-8156-3322-8

Library of Congress Control Number:
2013008331

MANUFACTURED IN THE UNITED STATES OF AMERICA

This volume is respectfully dedicated to
WILLIAM N. FENTON
Distinguished Professor of Anthropology Emeritus,
Dean of Iroquoianists, teacher, scholar, and trusted friend.

CHARLES T. GEHRING was born in Fort Plain, an old Revolutionary War and Erie Canal village in New York State's Mohawk Valley. After completing his undergraduate and graduate studies at Virginia Military Institute and West Virginia University, he continued post-graduate work with the assistance of a Fulbright grant at Albert-Ludwigs-Universität in Freiburg, Germany. There he began his study of the Dutch language and first realized his future research lay much closer to home. In 1973 he received a Ph.D. in Germanic Linguistics from Indiana University with a concentration in Netherlandic Studies. His dissertation was a linguistic investigation of the survival of the Dutch language in colonial New York. He is presently director of the New Netherland Research Center (sponsored by the New York State Library). The Center is responsible for translating the official records of the Dutch colony, promoting awareness of the Dutch role in American history, and maintaining a center for research in New Netherlandic studies at the Library. He has been a Fellow of the Holland Society of New York since 1979. In 1994, Her Majesty Queen Beatrix of the Netherlands conferred on him a knighthood as officer in the Order of Orange-Nassau. He has received gold medals from the Netherlands Society of Philadelphia, the Holland Society of New York, and the St. Nicholas Society of New York.

WILLIAM A. STARNA was born in Little Falls and raised in St. Johnsville, both Erie Canal towns in the Mohawk Valley. His undergraduate and graduate degrees are from the State University of New York at Albany. He is Professor Emeritus of Anthropology at the State University of New York College at Oneonta, and Adjunct Professor Emeritus of Geography, Queen's University, Kingston, Ontario. A longtime student of the Iroquoian and Algonquian peoples of eastern North America, in addition to federal–state–Indian relations, he has held a National Endowment for the Humanities Fellowship, a Senior Fellowship at the Nelson A. Rockefeller Institute of Government, and the Donald M. Blinken Fellowship in Academic Administration at SUNY Central Offices. He is the author of numerous scholarly articles and several books, most recently *From Homeland to New Land: A History of the Mahican Indians, 1600–1830* (2013).

GUNTHER MICHELSON (1924–2005) had a life-long interest in Iroquois history, culture, and linguistics. He was an expert in the Mohawk language and its documentation in historical sources.

CONTENTS

ILLUSTRATIONS

Preface to the Revised Edition

Our decision to produce a revised edition of the journal of Harmen Meyndertsz van den Bogaert, which was first published in 1988, was based on the usual considerations. There was the need to update the sources cited in our text and footnotes to reflect the most recent historical, ethnological, and archaeological literature on the Dutch and American Indian people relevant to seventeenth-century New Netherland; to refine, supplement, or edit a number of our annotations, some of which we judged to be superfluous and others which, in light of new data, were no longer current; and to correct typographical and stylistic slips along with the now and again gaffe that had found its way into the book. Taking advantage of the opportunity offered by Syracuse University Press to make these modifications, we also decided to broaden the historical context surrounding Van den Bogaert's journey, provide further background on the native residents of the region, and add to the biographical information on Van den Bogaert and his companions. Moreover, and completing the revision, we have included a transcription of the original Dutch-language journal.

Since the appearance of Van den Bogaert's journal, we have lost four valued colleagues who had generously assisted us in its publication. Robert Funk (1932–2002), New York State Archaeologist, and Temple University anthropologist Elisabeth Tooker (1927–2005) read our manuscript in its early stages, offering helpful advice. Our good friend Gunther Michelson (1924–2005) graciously authored the Mohawk language wordlist that Van den Bogaert had collected, and contributed the linguistic information found in the annotations. Our volume was dedicated, and remains so, to the distinguished scholar William N. Fenton (1908–2005).

We are grateful to Eileen M. McClafferty, who read and offered helpful comments on the final draft of our revision, and to Dietrich Gehring, who produced the accompanying map. We would also like to offer a special thank you to Leonard F. Tantillo of Schodack, New York, for permitting us to reproduce his most recent painting of Fort Orange, a "revision" of his first effort found on the cover of our 1988 book.

PREFACE TO THE FIRST EDITION

Hudson's historic voyage of 1609 to the New World was soon followed by a steady flow of traders from the Netherlands. It was only a matter of time before expeditions were sent into the interior to seek out precious metals or to treat with the Indians.

The first record of any Dutch exploration appears on an early map of New Netherland. The passage reports that in 1614 a trader named Kleyntjen traveled westward into the interior, then southward from the Maquas (Mohawks) along the New River (Susquehanna) to the Ogehage (Mohawk name for the Minquas or Susquehannocks). Although it is sparse information, it does represent the earliest account of Dutch explorations west of the Hudson River. If Kleyntjen kept a journal or wrote a report of his adventure, it has been lost. If other traders or employees of the West India Company ventured westward after Kleyntjen, their reports and accounts have also been lost, or disposed of in the great archival housecleaning of 1674, when the Company was reorganized.

It is ironic that the first detailed account of the Dutch in Iroquois country survived only because a copy of it fell into private hands. Without the Harmen Meyndertsz van den Bogaert journal, we would be deprived of the earliest known description of the Lower Iroquois and their environment, including detailed accounts of their settlements, healing rituals, systems of protocol, language, and subsistence practices. It stands as a unique and compelling document.

A translation of this type is inevitably indebted to many people and institutions. First and foremost we extend our gratitude to William N. Fenton, to whom this volume is dedicated. It was he who first introduced us to the journal and its value as a historic document many years ago. And it was he who encouraged us to complete the new translation and to produce the endnotes. This took more than the form of pats on the back. In 1976, he facilitated a request for a travel grant to the Huntington Library in San Marino, California, to examine the original document. In addition, he has listened to several papers we have presented on the journal, has discussed its contents with us, and has read our manuscript in draft form. Throughout, he has remained steadfast in his support and continued patience with our efforts.

We wish to thank Jack Campisi, Robert E. Funk, George Hamell, and Elisabeth Tooker, who read the manuscript in its several draft forms, offering helpful criticisms and suggestions.

We are also indebted to the Trustees of the Henry E. Huntington Library and Art Gallery for the research grant that made it possible to study the Van den Bogaert journal in its manuscript form.

A special note of appreciation goes to Leonard F. Tantillo of Schodack, New York, for allowing us to reproduce his painting *Fort Orange, 1635* in this work.

The map was drawn by Ronald E. Embling, Instructional Resource Center, State University of New York College at Oneonta. A facsimile page of the original document was prepared by Charles D. Winters, also of SUNY Oneonta. It is reproduced with the kind permission of the Huntington Library. In addition, Winters prepared the several plates found in our volume.

Finally, we would like to thank Ann Pasternak and Nancy A. M. Zeller for their assistance in preparing the manuscript.

The linguistic material contained in the endnotes was provided by Gunther Michelson of Montreal, Quebec, Canada. He also authored the Mohawk language wordlist and translations which follow the text of the journal and endnotes. His expert analysis of the language in the Indian passages and wordlist provides a new and important dimension to the journal which was lacking in any of the previous translations. We are grateful for his participation in this project and patient cooperation in the final production of this work. He is the best of colleagues, and we value his skills and friendship.

INTRODUCTION

$\mathfrak{I}$n 1621, the Dutch West India Company (Chartered West India Company, or *Geoctroyeerde Westindische Compagnie,* WIC) was chartered by the States General, the governing body of the United Provinces of the Netherlands. Its primary objective was to carry on the war with Spain in the Atlantic region following the expiration of the Twelve Years' Truce. The truce had been agreed to in 1609, after forty-one years of rebellion against the Habsburg Empire. This short interval, within what was to become known as the "Eighty Years' War" for independence, was used by the Dutch to develop and expand previously untapped world-wide markets and to explore for new and more economical trade routes on which to move its goods. Earlier, the Dutch East India Company (*Verenigde Oostindische Compagnie* or VOC), chartered in 1602, undertook a venture that had resulted in the United Provinces' claim to a huge expanse of territory in North America between New England and the English colonies on the Chesapeake, setting the scene for what would come.[1]

In 1609, when Henry Hudson, commanding a mixed Dutch and English crew aboard the VOC ship *Halve Maen,*

2. Pieter Goos's chart, with coat of arms (1666), from *Paskaerte van de Zuydt en Noordt Revier in Nieu Nederlandt Strechende van Capo Hinloopen tot Rechkewach ["Vignette"].*

sailed up the river now bearing his name, he was hoping to find a shorter and safer route to the Spice Islands in the Far East—the near-mythical Northwest Passage. Instead, he had happened upon the most well-situated access to the interior of North America and its riches south of New France. The importance of Hudson's discovery was soon realized by merchants in the Netherlands, who within a few short months after his return petitioned the States General for licenses authorizing them to exploit the resources of this region of the New World.

The resource that more than any other drew these merchants to the coast of America was the beaver. Current fashion in Europe required a steady flow of high quality pelts to be felted for the hat-making industry. According to preliminary explorations, there was every indication of an unlimited supply of this fur-bearing animal in what was soon to be called *Nieuw Nederlant* (New Netherland). The situation was perfect for any merchant interested in making a profit. The navigable North and South Rivers—the Hudson and the Delaware, respectively—afforded traders an easy and direct route inland. Here, posts might be established where the natives, seeking trade goods that, beginning in the mid-1500s, were available only from the St. Lawrence Valley, could bring their furs with a minimal amount of effort expended on both their and the merchants' part.[2] Thus, with the 1621 charter, the West India Company was given a monopoly over the fur trade in New Netherland, one that was built upon a network that had become established by private traders during the truce years. Now it was only necessary for the Company to refine the manner in which it would accumulate furs and to protect its interests.

The WIC was organized along the lines of the successful East India Company. As a stock operation with shareholders both large and small, its charter gave it the power to declare war on and to conclude agreements with the various indigenous peoples in its area of asserted economic jurisdiction, that is, from the west coast of Africa to the mid-Pacific. The Company had its own army and navy and was expected to make profits by capturing Spanish ships and capitalizing on the natural resources of the territories it claimed. Its governing body was known as the XIX, symbolizing the nineteen directors who came from

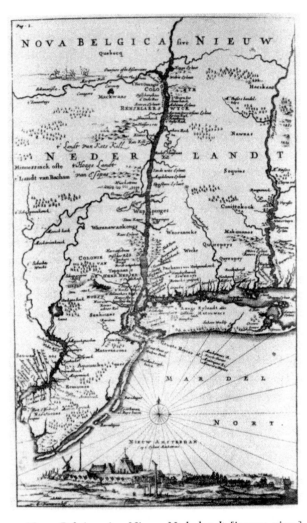

3. *Nova Belgica sivc Nieuw Nederlandt* [insert view] *Nieuw Amsterdam op t Eylant Manhattans* [The Van der Donck Map and View], 1651–1655, from *Beschryvinge Van Nieuw-Nederlandt.*

various regions of the United Provinces. The provinces of Holland and Zeeland held a controlling majority in the company, with representation by eight and six directors, respectively. Holland's interest was represented by the "chamber" at Amsterdam, which was responsible for the administration of affairs in New Netherland.[3]

In 1624, the Amsterdam chamber of the Company established trading houses on the three rivers that led into the interior of its claimed territory in North America: on High Island (now Burlington Island, New Jersey) in the Delaware River; at Fort Orange (Albany, New York) on the west bank of the Hudson River; and at Fort Hope (Hartford, Connecticut) on the Connecticut River. In the same year, thirty-two families arrived from *patria* to form agricultural communities near these posts as support for the fur-trading operations. A few were established on Nooten Eylandt (Nut Island), today's Governor's Island, off the southern tip of Manhattan.

The Company's first director, Willem Verhulst, arrived in the colony in 1625, with instructions to establish an administrative center on High Island, a decision based on the mistaken notion that its southern location would offer a climate conducive to year-round accessibility. He was also instructed to avoid any involvement in local Indian disputes. In 1626, however, Verhulst's commander at Fort Orange, Daniel van Crieckenbeeck, ignored this policy by siding with the Mahicans in a war with the Mohawks. The disastrous defeat of the Mahicans at the hands of what most consider to have been their traditional adversaries, including the death of the Dutch commander and several of his soldiers, led to a dangerous situation at the three fur-trading posts. The Mohawks, heavily outnumbering the Dutch, were in a position to take retaliatory measures by destroying the small communities in these remote areas, delivering a setback to Company operations from which it might not recover.[4]

This critical state of affairs was resolved by the new director, Peter Minuit (1580–1638), who replaced Verhulst in the spring of the same year after the latter had fallen into disfavor and was recalled to the Netherlands. In order to ensure the safety of the settlers, Minuit withdrew all of the families to the recently purchased Manhattan Island, where they were to establish support farms for what was now the Company's new center of operations.

Fort Orange and the other posts were maintained by a handful of soldiers while negotiations were carried out with the Mohawks. The Dutch apparently were able to assure the Mohawks that the actions against them were the decision of a local commander acting against orders. The Dutch negotiators, led by Pieter Barentsz, were not only able to appease the Mohawks, thus preventing retaliatory strikes against their vulnerable posts, but they also managed to establish a bond of mutual interest and friendship that was never broken. Dutch dependency on the Mohawks became so strong that in later years they were called upon to mediate Indian disputes as far away as the South River region of New Netherland. Moreover, these natives would serve as enforcers of Dutch interests against other Indians. The proximity of the Mohawks to

Fort Orange also discouraged potential competitors and adversaries, such as the French to the north and New Englanders to the east, from raiding this area, which was some 150 miles upriver from Manhattan and was cut off from any intended relief during the winter months.[5]

It was almost five years after the Crieckenbeeck disaster before the Dutch made any serious attempt to re-settle the Hudson Valley around Fort Orange. But now, rather than assume the added burden of colonization, the WIC yielded to the pressures of a faction of the directors who were in favor of promoting agricultural colonies in New Netherland by means of privately financed ventures called patroonships. Under this system, permitted by a concession to the WIC charter called the "Freedoms and Exemptions," WIC directors were authorized to negotiate with the natives to purchase large tracts of land. Private entrepreneurs — prospective patroons — were provided access to these holdings on the condition that they settle no less than fifty colonists there within a period of four years. And to avert any inside competition, it was further stipulated that these colonists were not to become involved in the fur trade.[6]

Patroonships were established from the Connecticut River to Delaware Bay. However, the only one that managed to survive was Rensselaerswijck, in which Kiliaen van Rensselaer (1586–1643), an Amsterdam jewelry merchant and WIC director, had a controlling interest.[7] His patroonship eventually contained almost one million acres of land on both sides of the Hudson River, approximately present-day Albany and Rensselaer counties. This land was purchased from numbers of Mahican Indians—for the Dutch, "the rightful owners"—with the WIC trading post of Fort Orange situated near its geographical center. The patroonship had its own court system and government, but it was ultimately responsible to the WIC. Capital crimes, for example, could be appealed to the court in New Amsterdam. During the administrations of the WIC directors Wouter van Twiller and Willem Kieft, Fort Orange and Rensselaerswijck were dependent on one another for survival, with the patroonship furnishing material and agricultural support to the Company's fur-trading operation, and the fort providing security for the colonists of Rensselaerswijck. By 1653, the Rensselaerswijck region, within which now stood the village of Beverwijck and its garrison, claimed to have 230 men capable of bearing arms.[8]

From the time the Dutch first established their colony, they had been acutely aware of French fur-trading operations in the St. Lawrence Valley. For their part, the Dutch had been trading with and supporting the Mohawks, who sat across the major trading route through the Mohawk Valley. The French, on the other hand, were in alliance with the Hurons, Ottawa Valley Algonquins, and the Montagnais, all of whom were in constant conflict with the Mohawks over control of the fur-rich St. Lawrence region. Thus, French attempts to gain access to the fur trade from the west and the environs of Oneida Lake—a back door to Iroquoia—became of major concern to the Dutch. If the French were permitted to negotiate a truce with the Iroquois and to establish a trading operation at Oneida, the Dutch fur-trading post at Fort Orange would become an anachronism and New Netherland would cease to be a viable and profitable investment for the WIC. It is in this context that Harmen Meyndertsz van den Bogaert was called upon to lead an expedition into Iroquois country.

In the winter of 1634, the commissary of Fort Orange, Marten Gerritsen, sent a party of three WIC employees west into the interior and toward the homelands of the five Iroquois nations. Their mission was to investigate the decline in the trade, a result, it had been concluded, of French incursions into Iroquoia. The intent was to negotiate a new price structure for the furs with the Indians, thus undercutting French competition and redirecting as much of the trade as possible back to Fort Orange.

The expedition consisted of Harmen Meyndertsz van den Bogaert, Jeronimus dela Croix, and Willem Thomassen. Unfortunately, only the latter two men are mentioned by name in the journal. When first made public in 1895, the journal's authorship was attributed to one Arent van Curler, a grandnephew of Kiliaen van Rensselaer and the founder of Schenectady, as well as a senior official of the patroonship. Nonetheless, it was later pointed out by A. J. F. van Laer, the archivist at the New York State Library, that Van Curler had not arrived in the colony until early 1638.[9] Van Laer suggested instead that Van den Bogaert was the leader of the party and the journal's author. He based this assertion on the fact that Van den Bogaert was employed as the barber-surgeon at Fort Orange during the 1630s. The journal itself implies that the author was a

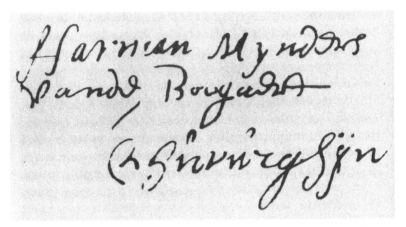

4. The signature of Harmen Meyndertsz van den Bogaert, Surgeon, from *The History of New Netherland* by E. B. O'Callaghan (D. Appleton and Co., New York, 1855).

surgeon because, on December 21, he was called upon to cure a sick Indian. He also exhibited an interest in Indian healing ceremonies. In addition to this, as is described later, in 1647 Van den Bogaert sought refuge in Iroquois country to avoid prosecution. It is not improbable that someone unfamiliar with the Mohawk Valley would have chosen to flee there; however, it does strengthen the case for presuming Van den Bogaert's authorship if we accept that he was escaping to a familiar territory.

Europeans who reached the coast of northeast North America beginning in the early sixteenth and continuing into the seventeenth century failed to discover a route through the continent or its northern waters to Asia. But they did find riches to their liking: first, the enormous supply of fish harvested from the Grand Banks of

Newfoundland, and then furs that were acquired from Indians with whom a brisk trade was carried out.

Although Portuguese, Basque, Breton, Norman, and English fishermen were among the first to sail to the region, they were preceded and followed by other, more purposeful and expansive explorations. Newfoundland was visited by John Cabot (Giovanni Caboto) in 1497, and again by Gaspar Côrte-Real in 1500. Giovanni da Verrazano wended his way along the east coast from North Carolina to Maine in 1524, while Estévan Gomez sailed the coast of New England, returning to Spain the next year with more than fifty Indian captives. Jacques Cartier explored the Gulf of St. Lawrence in 1534, and on his second voyage in 1535–1536, he carried out the earliest inland probe, ascending the St. Lawrence to the Indian towns of Stadacona (Quebec City) and Hochelaga (Montreal), revisiting the area in 1541–1542. It would be another sixty years, however, before Europeans once again ventured into the interior.[10]

From 1603 until his death in 1635, arguably the most celebrated European in northeastern North America was Samuel de Champlain. Explorer, soldier, ethnographer, and cartographer, among his other abilities, Champlain made more than twenty-five Atlantic crossings as he tirelessly promoted what David Hackett Fischer characterized as his "American project," leading to the founding of New France.[11] It was mere happenstance, however, that in the company of Huron, Algonquin, and Montagnais warriors, his violent encounter with a party of Mohawks at Lake Champlain took place in July 1609, a few days more than a month before Henry Hudson made his way upriver from Manhattan to near Albany. Short of the attack by Champlain and his Indian allies on a major Onondaga town in September 1615, there is no record of Europeans traveling into Iroquois country west of Fort Orange until Van den Bogaert's journey in 1634–1635.[12]

The Hudson, Housatonic, and Mohawk Valleys, all within what for the Dutch became New Netherland, were home to large numbers of native people. From western Long Island, northern New Jersey, and Manhattan Island, north into the Hudson Valley to near Catskill on the west side, and Germantown on the east, were communities of Munsees speaking an unknown number of dialects of Munsee, an Eastern Algonquian language. North of the Munsees, to the region just above Albany, and also in the upper reaches of the Housatonic Valley, were the Mahicans, speakers of at least two dialects of Mahican, also an Eastern Algonquian language. Both peoples practiced a mixed economy based on hunting, fishing, foraging for wild plant resources, and the planting of corn, beans, and squashes. As a reflection of their manner of subsistence, these Indians appear to have been relatively mobile, their small dispersed homesteads and camps suggesting seasonal occupations and adaptive flexibility and opportunism. Of the makeup of their settlements, however, little is known. At no time did individual Munsee or Mahican communities coalesce and form single political entities.

West of Fort Orange, past the confluence of Schoharie Creek and the Mohawk River and continuing up the valley to just beyond St. Johnsville, were the villages of the Mohawks. Along with the others of the five Iroquois nations—the Oneidas, Onondagas, Cayugas, and Senecas—they spoke Iroquoian, unrelated to the Eastern Algonquian languages that surrounded them. The Mohawks, along with their confederates, were heavily invested in labor-intensive farming, as evidenced by extensive fields of corn, beans, and squashes. This, in turn, compelled a commitment to sedentism, reflected in their densely populated, frequently palisaded, and politically autonomous towns. Hunting, fishing, and foraging completed the subsistence cycle.

On May 24, 1630, Van den Bogaert, an eighteen-year-old barber-surgeon, arrived in New Netherland aboard the West India Company ship *Eendracht.* There are no records of his early duties in the colony, although we know that he was posted to Fort Orange as Company surgeon the same year. His name next appears in testimony given before Cornelis van Tienhoven, the secretary of New Netherland on Manhattan, on September 1, 1638, where he states his age as twenty-six and his profession as surgeon. Thus, from this information, Van den Bogaert would have been only twenty-two years old when he began the expedition into Iroquois country, although a later document shows him to have been twenty.[13]

Besides his medical duties, Van den Bogaert was involved in other activities at Fort Orange and in the colony generally. Shortly after September 1638, he sailed as supercargo on the yacht *Canarivogel,* which took a prize

ship in the West Indies.[14] After his return to the colony the
following year, and before summer 1642, Van den Bogaert
married Jelisje Claesen, with whom there were four children. Later that year he was made commissary of stores on
Manhattan. It was probably the experience gained in this
office, in addition to his familiarity with the upper Hudson
region, that led to his appointment as commissary at Fort
Orange in 1645. Two years later, while still commissary, he
became part owner of the privateer *La Garce*.[15]

Nothing has been discovered of the lives of Van den
Bogaert's fellow travelers, Willem Thomassen and Jeronimus dela Croix, before their journey into the Mohawk Valley. Once back at Fort Orange, however, Dela Croix does
not appear in the record until May 1638, when, in a letter
to director Wouter van Twiller in New Amsterdam, Kiliaen
van Rensselaer offered this brief but important mention:
"*Ieronimus La Croix* has also communicated to me the cir-
cumstances of his journeys through the *maquans* land to
the *Sinnekens*."[16] That July, Dela Croix's name appears on
a list of recipients of disbursements following the death
of the trader Hendrick de Foreest. The next year he was
granted power of attorney to represent one of the colony's citizens in the collection of a debt, a task he under-
takes again in 1643, and for three others in 1644. Then
silence.[17] Thomassen, it seems, was a career seaman who
purchased a home and garden on Long Island in 1643.
At the time he was pilot of the yacht *Pauwe*. In 1646 he
skippered the *Jager*, and by August 1647, he was master of
Valckenier. He is last mentioned, while still in command of
this ship, two years later.[18]

Van den Bogaert's career took a sudden turn in fall 1647, when he fled into the Mohawk Valley to avoid answering a charge of sodomy committed with his black servant Tobias. Taking refuge with the same people he had visited thirteen years before, where he was said to be "living as an Indian," he found himself pursued by Hans Vos, assigned the task of his capture by the court at Fort Orange. Cornered by Vos in an Indian house, Van den Bogaert reportedly set it ablaze in an unsuccessful attempt to cover his escape. Soon apprehended, he was returned to Fort Orange to await the resolution of his case.[19]

The whole affair was considered so important that an Indian messenger was sent overland to New Amsterdam in order to inform the new director, Petrus Stuyvesant, of these events. Stuyvesant, after receiving a complaint from the Indians regarding their losses of provisions, pelts, and sewant in the fire, decided in council to offer them compensation by selling Van den Bogaert's garden plot on Manhattan and turning over the proceeds. He then delayed a final resolution of the case until additional information could be secured from Fort Orange in the spring. However, before the communication link could be reestablished by ship with Fort Orange, Van den Bogaert escaped imprisonment. As he ran over the frozen river to avoid recapture by soldiers from the fort, the ice broke underneath him and he was drowned.[20]

The journal is composed of rag paper leaves, each measuring 14 x 12 1/8 inches (47 cm. x 37 cm.). Each leaf is folded in half to form four pages. Nine leaves are sewn together with white thread to make a total of thirty-six pages, thirty-two of which contain the journal entries and a Mohawk-Dutch vocabulary. The paper itself exhibits a watermark identified as the "Arms of Baden Hochberg," which establishes it as Rhenish-made paper. The first page, which serves as the front cover, carries the notation "No. R." This follows the Dutch record-keeping system of using alphabetical letters as reference marks. When single letters were exhausted, they were doubled, then tripled, and so forth.

The handwriting is clear and shows the careful execution of a clerk or secretary trained in recording and copying records. Errors in the text indicate that it was copied from Van den Bogaert's original. In several instances it is obvious that the copyist was uncertain of the handwriting he was transcribing. Where the context made it obvious that he was in error, he corrected himself. At other times the errors were retained. Such scribal errors would not have been made by the person who kept the original. We assume, therefore, that shortly after Van den Bogaert's return to Fort Orange, a copy was made at the request of officials in Rensselaerswijck.

Although during this period of time Kiliaen van Rensselaer was prohibited by the "Freedoms and Exemptions" from engaging in the fur trade, he did monitor it carefully and would have been extremely interested in the negotiations Van den Bogaert had conducted with the Iroquois. Any intrusions by the French in the fur trade, he knew, would have had a direct impact on his properties along the Hudson, not to mention his considerable investments in the colony. We believe that the copy of the journal was sent to Kiliaen van Rensselaer in Amsterdam to inform his personal and business affairs. There it must have remained among his papers, eventually finding its way into private hands, when in 1895 it was discovered and purchased by General James Grant Wilson. The location of the original journal is unknown; however, it is possible that it became part of the extensive records of the West India Company archives in Amsterdam, which were disposed of in 1674 when the Company was reorganized.

The history of the manuscript and its ultimate acquisition by the Henry E. Huntington Library in San Marino, California, is an interesting account in itself. Wilson states that the journal was discovered and obtained by him in the summer of 1895 while in Holland, and soon thereafter translated and published in *The Independent,* appearing the next year in the American Historical Association's annual report.[21] J. Franklin Jameson, acknowledging Wilson's discovery, believed that the copy was identical to that mentioned by Nicolaas de Roever, the late archivist of the city of Amsterdam, as being among the papers of the patroon, Van Rensselaer.[22]

General James Grant Wilson (1832–1914) was born in Edinburgh, Scotland. One year later, his family emigrated to the United States, taking up residence in Poughkeepsie, New York. Following his education, Wilson moved to Chicago, where he edited and published a number of periodicals. In 1862, he was commissioned an officer in the 15th Illinois Cavalry and later the 4th United States Colored

Cavalry, seeing action in several campaigns in the Mississippi Valley. He resigned his commission in 1865, living the remainder of his life in New York City. His writings were prolific, consisting mainly of biographies. He held memberships in a number of professional organizations including the American Ethnological Society (President, 1900–1914) and the American Authors' Guild (President, 1892–1899).

Following the journal's initial publication in *The Independent*, Wilson appears to have sold the manuscript. William M. Beauchamp (1830–1925), an early and noted student of the Iroquois, mentions in a letter to Samuel L. Frey (1833–1924), a historian of the Mohawk Valley, the fact that by 1908 Wilson no longer had the journal but only the translation he had made. Also corresponding with Frey was Myron F. Westover, a past president of the Schenectady Historical Society. He informed Frey that the journal had been purchased by a "Mr. White" for $800, a considerable sum at the time. Apparently, Westover was first told of the existence of the manuscript by Dr. William Elliott Griffis (1843–1928), a former pastor of the First Reformed Church in Schenectady, who also indicated that the owner was a "Mr. White" from Brooklyn. "Mr. White" was William Augustus White (1843–1927), a wealthy manufacturer, bibliophile, and collector, and a close friend of a vice-president of General Electric, which was headquartered in Schenectady. At Westover's request, he brought the journal to Schenectady, where it was shown to A. J. F. van Laer (1869–1955), the previously mentioned archivist and translator of Dutch.[23] The fact of White's ownership

5. The first page of Van den Bogaert's journal.
HM 819. Bogaert, Harmen Meynderstz van den.
"Journals of Travels in NY, 1634–1635." Reproduced by permission of The Huntington Library, San Marino, California.

is further strengthened by the presence of the initials "W. A. W." pencilled in the lower right corner of the otherwise blank verso of the title page of the journal.

Sometime after 1908, Henry E. Huntington (1850–1927), the railroad executive and financier, procured the original manuscript. Today it is in the collections of his library in San Marino, California, cataloged as HM 819. There are no acquisition records regarding the journal, nor is there any other information as to how it was obtained. A library official suspects that it was acquired during Huntington's lifetime, when record keeping on the provenance of manuscripts was sometimes less than adequate.

To the best of our knowledge, Wilson's translation of the manuscript is the first. A revision appears in Jameson's volume, completed by S.G. Nissensen from the original copy.[24] Ours is the third.

NOTES

1. See generally Boxer, *Dutch Seaborne Empire*, and Israel, *Dutch Republic*.

2. See Pendergast, "Introduction of European Goods."

3. On the West India Company and the founding of New Netherland, including authoritative treatments of the economic, political, social, religious, and administrative developments in the colony, see Rink, *Holland on the Hudson*, and Jacobs, *New Netherland*. See also Hart, *New Netherland Company*; Bachman, *Peltries or Plantations*.

4. For a thorough treatment of this conflict, see Starna and Brandão, "Mohawk-Mahican War." The estimated Mohawk population at this time was over 7,000 (Snow, *Iroquois*, 96, 110).

5. On Mohawk-Dutch political interaction, see Richter, *Ordeal of the Longhouse*; Jennings, *Ambiguous Iroquois Empire*; Dennis, *Landscape of Peace*; and Starna, *Homeland to New Land*.

6. See Jacobs, *New Netherland*, 113–14, on the Freedoms and Exemptions.

7. See Venema, *Kiliaen van Rensselaer*. On the patroonships, see Rink, *Holland on the Hudson*, 94–116, and Jacobs, *New Netherland*, 112–32.

8. Gehring, "Van Rensselaer Letter," 28. On the founding and growth of the village that would become Albany, see Venema, *Beverwijck*.

9. Van Laer, trans. and ed., *Van Rensselaer Bowier Manuscripts*, 26, 271n14, 817.

10. On a history of European explorations to the region, see Brasser, "Early Indian-European Contacts."

11. Fischer, *Champlain's Dream*, 6.

12. Fischer, *Champlain's Dream*, 327–34.

13. O'Callaghan, *Register of New Netherland*, 124; Van Laer, trans. and ed., *New York Historical Manuscripts*, 1:54, 271, 2:194.

14. Van Laer, trans. and ed., *New York Historical Manuscripts*, 1:60–61, 4:59.

15. O'Callaghan, *Register of New Netherland*, 31, 48; Van Laer, trans. and ed., *New York Historical Manuscripts*, 2:436–37.

16. Van Laer, trans. and ed., *Van Rensselaer Bowier Manuscripts*, 401. It is not known whether Dela Croix had sailed back to Amsterdam to personally deliver the journal to Van Rensselaer or had it sent by courier.

17. Van Laer, trans. and ed., *New York Historical Manuscripts*, 1:79, 140, 2:176, 248–49, 253.

18. Van Laer, trans. and ed., *New York Historical Manuscripts*, 2:101, 322, 476–77, 4:383, 3:151–52.

19. Reporting on what he had heard but not witnessed of the incident, Govert Loockermans, a merchant and one of the Nine Men, an advisory body to the director, said that Van den Bogaert had been involved with two servants (Loockermans to Gillis Verbrugge, Dec. 21, 1647). See also Van Laer, trans. and ed., *New York Historical Manuscripts*,

4:480–81; Van Laer, trans. and ed., *Minutes of the Court*, 105; Gehring, trans. and ed., *Delaware Papers*, 22 (quotation).

20. Based on the second-hand information he had received, Loockermans concluded that Van den Bogaert had committed suicide, an unlikely scenario (Loockermans to Gillis Verbrugge, Mar. 28, 1648). Van den Bogaert's escape may have been made easy by that winter's high waters, which had "almost entirely washed away" parts of the fort (Van Laer, trans. and ed., *New York Historical Manuscripts*, 4:550; O'Callaghan and Fernow, eds., *Documents Relative*, 14:92–93).

21. See Wilson, "Corlaer and His Journal" and "Arent Van Curler."

22. Jameson, ed., *Narratives*, 137; Van Laer, trans. and ed., *Van Rensselaer Bowier Manuscripts*, 26.

23. For the information detailed in this paragraph, see Frey Papers.

24. Jameson, ed., *Narratives*, 137–62.

The Journal of
Harmen Meyndertsz
van den Bogaert

Praise God above all. At Fort Orange, 1634.

11 December. Report of the most important things that happened to me while traveling to the Maquasen and Sinnekens.[1] First of all, the reasons why we went were that the Maquasen and Sinnekens had often come to our Commissary Marten Gerritsen[2] and me, saying that there were French Indians in their country, and that they had called a truce with them, so that they, namely, the Maquasen, would trade furs with them there, because the Maquasen wanted as much for their furs as did the French Indians.[3] Therefore, I asked Sr. Marten Gerritsen's permission to go there and learn the truth of the matter in order to report to their High Mightinesses[4] as soon as possible, because trade was going very badly. So for these reasons I went with Jeromus la Croex and Willem Tomassen. May the Lord bless our journey.

Between 9 and 10 o'clock we left with 5 Maquasen Indians mostly toward the northwest,[5] and at 1/2 hour into the evening, after eight miles,[6] we came to a hunter's cabin, where we spent the night by the waterway that runs into their country and is named Oÿoge.[7] The Indians fed us venison here. The country is mostly covered with pine trees and there is much flat land. This waterway flows past their castle[8] in their country, but we were unable to travel on it because of the heavy flooding.

12 ditto. We continued our journey 3 hours before dawn. The Indians, who traveled with us, would have left us there, if I had not noticed it; and when we intended to eat something, their dogs had eaten up our meat and cheese so that we had nothing but dry bread to travel on. After we had traveled an hour, we came to the tributary that flows into our river and past the Maquase's villages.[9] Here there was a heavy ice flow. Jeronimus crossed first in a canoe made of tree bark with an Indian because only 2 men could travel together in it.[10] After this Willem and I [crossed]. It was so dark that we could not see one another without staying close together so that it was not without danger. After crossing over, we went another 1 1/2 miles and came to a hunter's cabin.[11] We entered and ate some venison there. We then continued our journey. After we had gone another 1/2 mile, we saw some people coming toward us. When they saw us, they ran away. Throwing down their bags and packs, they ran into a marsh and hid behind a thicket so that we were unable to see them. We looked at their goods and packs, taking a small loaf of bread baked with beans.[12] We ate it up and continued on mostly along this aforesaid waterway, which flowed most fiercely because of the flood. There are many islands in this waterway, on the banks of which are 500 or 600 *morgens* of flatland; indeed, much more.[13] When we had

Map of the Mohawk Valley and Environs

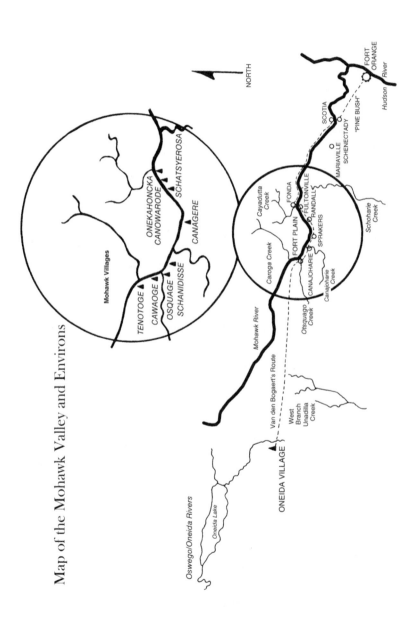

covered, by estimation, 11 miles, we came at one hour into the evening to a cabin 1/2 mile from the first castle.[14] No one was there but women. We would have then continued on, but I could not move my feet because of the rough going; so, we slept there. It was very cold, with a north wind.

13 ditto. In the morning we went together to the castle over the ice that had frozen in the waterway during the night. When we had gone 1/2 mile, we came into their first castle, which stood on a high hill.[15] There were only 36 houses, row on row in the manner of streets, so that we easily could pass through. These houses are constructed and covered with the bark of trees, and are mostly flat above. Some are 100, 90, or 80 steps long; 22 or 23 feet high.[16] There were also some interior doors made of split planks furnished with iron hinges. In some houses we also saw ironwork: iron chains, bolts, harrow teeth, iron hoops, spikes, which they steal when they are away from here.[17] Most of the people were out hunting for bear and deer. These houses were full of grain that they call ONESTI and we corn; indeed, some held 300 or 400 skipples.[18] They make boats and barrels of tree-bark, and sew with it. We ate here many baked and boiled pumpkins which they called ANONSIRA.[19] None of the chiefs was at home, except for the most principal one, called ADRI-OCHTEN, who was living 1/4 mile from the fort in a small cabin because many Indians here in the castle had died of smallpox.[20] I invited him to come visit with me, which he did. He came and bade me welcome, and said that he wanted us to come with him very much. We would have

gone, but we were called by another chief when we were already on the path, and turned back toward the castle. He had a large fire started at once, and a fat haunch of venison cooked, from which we ate; and he also gave us 2 bearskins to sleep on, and presented me with three beaver pelts.[21] In the evening I made some cuts with a knife on Willem Tomassen's leg, which had swollen from walking, and then smeared it with bear's grease. We slept here in this house, and ate large quantities of pumpkin, beans, and venison, so that we suffered of no hunger here but fared as well as it is possible in their country. I hope that everything shall succeed.

14 ditto. Jeronimus wrote a letter to the commissary, Marten Gerritsen, asking for paper, salt, and ATSOCH-WAT, i.e., Indian tobacco.[22] We went out with the chief to see if we could shoot some turkeys, but got none. However, in the evening I bought a very fat turkey for 2 hands of sewant,[23] which the chief cooked for us; and the grease that cooked from it he put in our beans and corn.[24] This chief let me see his idol which was a marten's head with protruding teeth, covered with red duffel-cloth.[25] Others keep a snake, a turtle, a swan, a crane, a pigeon, and such similar objects for idols or for telling fortunes; they think that they will then always have luck.[26] 2 Indians left from here for Fort Orange with skins.

15 ditto. I went out again with the chief to hunt turkeys, but we got none. In the evening the chief once again let us see his idol. On account of the heavy snow over the path we decided to stay here another 2 or 3 days until the opportunity presented itself to proceed.

16 ditto. In the afternoon a good hunter named SICK-ARIS came here who wanted us to go with him very much and carry our goods to his castle. He offered to let us sleep in his house and stay there as long as we pleased. Because he offered us so much, I presented him with a knife and two awls; and to the chief in whose home we had stayed I presented a knife and a scissors.[27] Then we departed from this castle ONEKAHONCKA.[28] After we had gone 1/2 mile over the ice we saw a village with only 6 houses. It was called CANOWARODE,[29] but we did not enter it because he said it was not worth much. After we had gone another 1/2 mile we passed a village with 12 houses called SCHAT-SYEROSY.[30] This one was like the other, saying also that it was not worth much. After we had gone 1 mile or a mile and a half past great tracts of flatland, we entered a castle at about 2 hours in the evening. I could see nothing else but graves.[31] This castle is called CANAGERE and is situated on a hill without palisades or any defense.[32] There were only 7 men at home, and a group of old women and children.[33] The chiefs of this castle TONNOSATTON and TONIWEROT[34] were out hunting so that we slept in SECKARIS'S house as he had promised us. We counted in his house 120 pelts of marketable beaver that he had caught with his own hands.[35] We ate beaver meat here every day. In this castle there are 16 houses, 50, 60, 70, 80 steps long, and one of 16 steps, and one of five steps in which a bear was being fattened. It had been in there almost 3 years and was so tame that it ate everything given it.[36]

17 ditto. Sunday. We looked over our goods and came upon a paper of sulphur. Jeronimus took some out and

threw it on the fire. They saw the blue flame and smelled the odor, and told us that they also had such goods. When SICKARIS came in, they got it out and let us look at it, and it was the same. We asked him how he came by it. He told us that they got it from the foreign Indians, and that they considered it good for healing many illnesses, but principally for their legs when they became very sore from traveling and are very tired.[37]

18 ditto. 3 women came here from the Sinnekens with some dried and fresh salmon, but they smelled very bad. They sold each salmon for one guilder or 2 hands of sewant. They also brought much green tobacco to sell, and had been 6 days underway. They could not sell all their salmon here, but went with it to the first castle.[38] Then we were supposed to travel with them when they returned. In the evening Jeronimus told me that an Indian was planning to kill him with a knife.

December 19. We received a letter from Marten Gerritsen dated the eighteenth of this year.[39] With it came paper, salt, and tobacco for the Indians and a bottle of brandy. We hired a man to guide us to the Sinnekens, and gave him 1/2 piece of duffel, 2 axes, 2 knives, and 2 awls. If it had been summer there would have been people enough to accompany us, but since it was winter they did not want to leave their country because it snowed there often a man's height deep. Today we had a very heavy rain. I gave this Indian a pair of shoes. His name was SQORHEA.[40]

December 20. Then we left the second castle, and when we had gone 1 mile our Indian SQORHEA came before a stream that we had to cross. This stream was running very hard with many large chunks of ice, because yesterday's heavy rain had broken up the stream so that we were in great danger. Had one of us just fallen, it would have been the end. But the Lord God protected us and we made it across. We were soaked up to the waist.[41] After going another half mile, with wet and frozen clothing, stockings, and shoes, we came to a very high hill on which stood 32 houses, all similar to the previous ones. Some were 100, 90, 80 steps or paces long. In each house there were 4, 5, or 6 places for fires and cooking. There were many Indians at home here so that we caused much curiosity in the young and old; indeed, we could hardly pass through the Indians here. They pushed one another into the fire to see us. It was almost midnight before they left us. We could not do anything without having them shamelessly running about us. This is the third castle, and it is called SCHANIDISSE. The chief's name is TEWOWARY.[42] This evening I got a lion skin to cover myself with; however, in the morning I had at least 100 lice.[43] We ate here much venison. There is considerable flatland around and near this castle, and the woods are full of oak and walnut trees. We got a beaver here in exchange for an awl.

December 21. We left very early in the morning, intending to go to the fourth castle. However, after we had gone a half mile we came to a village with nine houses called OSQUAGE. The chief's name was OQUOHO, i.e., wolf.[44] Here there was a great stream which our guide would not cross. Because of the heavy rain, the water was over our heads.[45] For this reason we delayed until Saturday. This

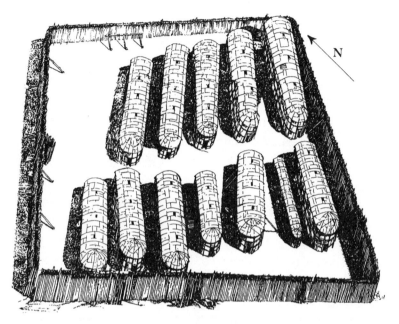

6. Artist's depiction of the Mohawk village of Caughnawaga, c. 1666/7–1693, from the drawing by A. H. van Vliet, with permission of the National Kateri Tekakwitha Shrine, Fonda, N.Y.

chief gave us many goods and fed us well, for everything in his house was at our disposal. He told me simply that I was his brother and good friend. Indeed, he also told me how he had traveled thirty days overland, and saw there an Englishman coming from the Minquas in order to learn their language for the fur trade.[46] I asked him whether there were French Indians near the Sinnekens. He said yes, and I was pleased, and thought that I would then reach my objective. I was asked here to heal a man who was very sick.[47]

December 22. In the morning at sunrise we crossed the stream together. It was over our knees and was so cold that our stockings and shoes quickly froze as hard as armor-plate. The Indians dared not cross there, but went 2 by 2 with a stick from hand to hand. After we had gone 1/2 mile, we came to a village called CAWAOGE.[48] It had 14 houses and a tame bear. We went in and smoked a pipe of tobacco because the old man, who was our guide, was very tired. An old man came to us and said, "Welcome, welcome, should you have to stay overnight." However, we left in order to continue our journey. I wanted to buy the bear, but they would not part with it. All along the path stood many trees very similar to the savin tree. They have a very thick bark.[49] This village is also located on a high hill. After we had gone a mile overland through a sparsely wooded region we came to the 4th castle, called TENOTOGE.[50] It had 55 houses some 100 steps [in length], and others more or less as large. The waterway that was mentioned earlier ran past here and took the course mostly northwest and southeast. There are more houses on the opposite bank of the waterway; however, we did not enter them because they were mostly full of grain.[51] The houses in this castle are full of grain and beans. Here the Indians looked on in amazement; for most everyone was at home, and they crowded in on us so much that we could barely pass among them.[52] After a long period, an Indian came to us who took us to his house and we went into it. The castle was surrounded with 3 rows of palisades. However, now there were only 6 or 7 [posts] left, so thick that it was unbelievable that Indians could do it.[53] They pushed one another into the fire in order to see us.

23 Dec. A man came shouting and screaming through some of the houses here. However, we did not know what it was supposed to mean. After a while Jeronimus de la Croix came, and wondered what it meant that the Indians were arming themselves. I asked them what was meant by it and they said [it was] nothing against me, "We are going to play with one another." There were four with clubs, and some with axes and sticks, so that there were 20 men under arms; 9 on one side and 11 on the other. Then they went at each other, fighting and striking. Some wore armor and helmets which they made themselves from thin reeds and cord woven together so that no arrow or axe could penetrate to cause serious injury.[54] After they had skirmished in this manner for a long time, the adversaries ran at one another; and the one dragged the other by the hair as they would do with conquered enemies, and would then cut their heads off.[55] They wanted us to fire our pistols, but we went away and left them.[56] Today we feasted on 2 bears, and we received today 1/2 skipple of beans and some dried strawberries.[57] Also, we provided ourselves here with bread that we could take along on the journey. Some of it had nuts, chestnuts, dried blueberries, and sunflower seeds baked in it.[58]

24 Dec. Since it was Sunday I looked in on a person who was sick. He had invited into his house 2 of their doctors who were supposed to heal him. They were called SUNACHKOES.[59] As soon as they arrived, they began to sing, and kindled a large fire, sealing the house all around so that no draft could enter. Then both of them put a snakeskin around their heads and washed their hands

and faces. They then took the sick person and laid him before the large fire. Taking a bucket of water in which they had put some medicine, they washed a stick in it 1/2 ell long.[60] They stuck it down their throats so that the end could not be seen, and vomited on the patient's head and all over his body. Then they performed many farces with shouting and rapid clapping of hands, as is their custom, with much display, first on one thing and then on the other, so that the sweat rolled off them everywhere.[61]

25 Dec. As it was Christmas Day, we arose early in the morning, intending to go to the Sinnekens. However, on account of the steady snow we were unable to start out, because no one would go with us to carry our goods. I asked them how many chiefs there were and they told me 30 persons.

26 Dec. This morning I was given 2 pieces of bear meat to take on the journey. We took our leave amid much uproar that surged behind and before us. They repeatedly shouted: "ALLESE RONDADE," i.e., "Shoot!"[62] However, we did not want to shoot. Finally they went away. Today we passed over much flatland, and also through a stream over our knees in depth. I think that we proceeded today mostly in a west-northwest direction. The woods through which we traveled were at first mostly oak, but after 3 or 4 hours underway we encountered mostly birch. It snowed the entire day so that it was very difficult to climb over the hills. After an estimated seven miles, we came to a bark hut in the woods where we kindled a fire and stayed the night. It continued to snow with a strong north wind. It was extremely cold.

Dec. 27. Early in the morning we continued on with great difficulty through 2 1/2 feet of snow in some places. We went over hills, and through thickets, seeing tracks of many bear and elk, but no Indians.[63] Here there are beech trees. After going 7 or 8 miles, we found at sunset once again a hut in the woods with little bark, but with some tree branches. We again made a big fire and cooked SAPPAEN.[64] It was so cold during the night that I could barely sleep two hours.

Dec. 28. We continued on, proceeding as before.[65] After we had gone 1 or 2 miles, we came to a waterway that the Indians told me flowed into the land of the Minquasen. After having gone another mile we came to another waterway that flowed into the South River, so the Indians told me.[66] Here many otters and beavers were caught.[67] Today we passed over many high hills. The woods are full of many large trees, but mostly birch. After going another 7 or 8 miles, we did as above. It was extremely cold.

Dec. 29. We pushed on with our journey. After having traveled a while, we came to a very high hill. When we had just about reached the top, I fell so that I thought that I had broken my ribs; however, it was only the handle of my sword that had broken. We passed through low lands where many oak trees and ironwood grew.[68] After 7 more miles, we found another hut into which we settled ourselves. We made a fire and ate up all the food we had, for the Indians said that we were still about 4 miles from the castle. It was nearly sunset when another Indian ran on to the castle to tell them that we were coming. We would have gone too, but because we were all very hungry the Indians would not take us along. Course NW.

Dec. 30. We proceeded toward the Sinnekens' castle without eating. After having gone a while, the Indians pointed out to me the tributary of the river before Fort Orange, which passes through the land of the Maquaesen.[69] A woman came along the way, bringing us baked pumpkins to eat. This stretch is mostly full of birch wood and flatlands cleared for sowing. Just before reaching the castle, we saw 3 graves in the manner of our graves: long and high. Otherwise, their graves are round. These graves were surrounded with palisades that they had split from trees, and were so neatly made that it was a wonder. They were painted red, white, and black. Only the chief's grave had an entrance, above which stood a large wooden bird surrounded by paintings of dogs, deer, snakes, and other animals.[70] After having gone 4 or 5 miles, the Indians asked us to shoot. We fired our weapons, which we reloaded, and then we went to the castle. Northwest of us we saw a very large body of water. Opposite the water was extremely high ground which seemed to lie in the clouds.[71] When I inquired about it, the Indians told me that the French came into that water to trade.[72] After that we confidently went to the castle, where the Indians divided themselves into 2 rows and let us pass in between them through their entrance.[73] The one we passed through was 3 1/2 feet wide. Above the entrance stood 3 large wooden images, carved as men, by which 3 locks fluttered that they had cut from the heads of slain Indians as a token of truth, that is to say, victory. This castle has 2 entrances,

one on the east and one on the west side. A lock was also
hanging by the east gate, but this gate was 1 1/2 half feet
smaller than the other. Then we were finally brought into
the farthest house, where I found many acquaintances.
We were put in the place where the chief was accustomed
to sit because he was not home at the time. We were cold,
wet, and tired. We received food immediately, and they
built a good fire. This castle is also located on a very high
hill and was surrounded with 2 rows of palisades, 767
steps in circumference, in which there are 66 houses, but
built much better and higher than all the others.[74] There
were many wooden gables on the houses which were
painted with all sorts of animals.[75] They sleep here mostly
on raised platforms, more than any other Indians. In the
afternoon, one of the councillors came to ask me what we
were doing in his country and what we brought him for
gifts.[76] I said that we brought him nothing, but that we
just came for a visit. However, he said that we were worth
nothing because we brought him no gifts.[77] Then he told
how the French had traded with them here with 6 men
and had given them good gifts; for they had traded in
the aforementioned river last August of this year with six
men.[78] We saw there good timber axes, French shirts, coats,
and razors. And this councillor derided us as scoundrels,
and said that we were worthless because we gave them so
little for their furs. They said that the French gave them
six hands of sewant for one beaver and all sorts of other
things in addition. The Indians sat so close to us here that
we could barely sit. If they had wanted to do anything to
us we could have done nothing, but there was no danger

to our persons. In this river already mentioned, there are 6 or 7 or even 800 salmon caught in one day. I saw houses with 60, 70, and more dried salmon.[79]

31 Dec. On Sunday the chief of this castle returned home. He was called ARENIAS. He came with another man, saying that they came from the French Indians. Some of the Indians gave a scream, saying JAWE ARENIAS, which meant that they thanked him for coming.[80] I told him that we would fire 3 shots this evening, and they said that it was good and they were very pleased. We asked them for the locations of all of their castles and for their names, and how far they were from one another. They put down kernels of corn and stones, and Jeronimus made a map from them. We reckoned everything in miles; how far each place was from another. The Indians here told us that in that high country that we had seen near the lake there lived people with horns.[81] They also said that many beavers were caught there; however, they dared not travel so far because of the French Indians. For this reason, therefore, they would make peace. This evening we fired 3 shots in honor of the year of our Lord and Redeemer Jesu Cristo.

PRAISE THE LORD ABOVE ALL

IN THE CASTLE ONNEYUTTEHAGE

OR SINNEKENS   1635 January[82]

1 January. An Indian once again called us scoundrels, as has been previously told, and he was very malicious so that Willem Tomassen became so angry that the tears ran from his eyes. The Indian, seeing that we were

upset, asked us why we looked at him with such anger. We were sitting during this time with their 46 persons around and near us. Had they had any malicious intentions, they could have easily grabbed us with their hands and killed us without much trouble. However, when I had heard his screaming long enough, I told him that he was the scoundrel. He began to laugh and said that he was not angry and said "You must not be angry. We are happy that you have come here." Jeronimus gave the chief 2 knives, 2 scissors, and some awls and needles that we had with us. In the evening the Indians hung up a belt of sewant and some other strung sewant that the chief had brought back from the French Indians as a token of peace that the French Indians were free to come among them; and they sang HO SCHENE JO HO HO SCHENE I ATSIEHOENE ATSIHOENE. Whereupon all the Indians shouted 3 times NETHO NETHO NETHO, and then hung up another belt, singing KATON KATON KATON KATON. Then they shouted in a loud voice HŸ HŸ HŸ.[83] After long deliberation they concluded the peace for 4 years, and then each went to his house.[84]

Jan. 2. The Indians came to us and said that we had to wait another 4 or 5 days; and if we could not go sooner, then they would provide us with all necessities. However, I said that we could not wait long. They answered that they had sent for the ONNEDAEGES, which is the castle next to them.[85] But I said that they mostly let us starve, whereupon they said that henceforth we would receive sufficient food. Today we were twice invited to feast on bear meat and salmon.

January 3. Some old men came to us and said that they wanted to be our friends, and that we must not be afraid. Whereupon I told them that we were not afraid. Toward midday they gathered their council here with 24 men. After they had conferred for a long time, an old man came to me and felt whether my heart was beating against his hand. When he shouted that we were not afraid, 6 more men came from the council, and they presented us with a beaver coat. They gave it to me saying, "It is for your journey, because you are so tired." And pointing to my feet and his, said, "That is also because you have walked through the snow." When we accepted it, they shouted 3 times NETHO NETHO NETHO, which means that they were pleased. At once they laid 5 more beaver skins at my feet, and thereby requested that they would like to have 4 hands of sewant and 4 hands of long cloth[86] for each large beaver because "We have to travel so far with our pelts and when we arrive we often find no cloth, no sewant, no axes, kettles, or anything else; and thus we have labored in vain. Then we have to go back a long way carrying our goods."[87] After we had sat for a time, an old man came to us for whom they translated us in another language, and he said, "You have not said whether we shall have 4 hands or not."[88] Whereupon I told him that we had no authority to promise them that, but that we would tell the chief at the Manhatas, who was our commander, and that I would inform him of everything in the spring, and come myself into their country.[89] Then they said to me WELSMACHKOO, "You must not lie, and come in the spring to us and bring us all an answer.[90] If we receive

4 hands, then we shall trade our pelts with no one else."
Then they gave me the 5 beavers and shouted again in a
loud voice NETHO NETHO NETHO; and so that everything should be firm and binding, they shouted or sang:
HA ASSIRONI ATSIMACHKOO KENT OYAKAYING
WEE ONNEYATTE ONAONDAGE KOYOCKWE HOO
SENOTO WANYAGWEGANNE HOO SCHENEHALA-
TON KASTEN KANOSONI YNDICKO, which was to
say that I should go to all these places, by naming all the
castles, and I would go there freely and be free there in
every place; I would have house and fire, wood, and anything else.[91] Whatever I received there would be mine;
and if I wished to go to the French, then they would go
with me and bring me back wherever I desired. There-
upon they again shouted in a loud voice 3 times, NETHO
NETHO NETHO, and I was again made a present of a
beaver. This day we were invited to eat bear meat. In this
chief's house 3 or 4 meals were eaten every day. Whatever
was not cooked there was brought in from other houses
in large kettles, because the council came here every day
to eat; and whoever is in the house receives a wooden bowl
full of food, for it is the custom that every man who comes
here receives a bowl full. If bowls are lacking, then they
bring their own bowls and spoons. They then sit down next
to one another where the bowls are fetched and brought
back full, because an invited guest does not stand up until
he has eaten. Sometimes they sing and sometimes not.
They then thank the host and each returns home.

Jan. 4. Two men came to me and said that I should
come and see how they would drive out the devil; but I

7. *t'Fort nieuw Amsterdam op de Manhatans* [The Hartgers View of
Manhattan], 1626–1628, from *Beschrijvinghe Van Virginia Nieuw
Nederlandt,* Amsterdam.

said that I had seen that before. However, I had to go
along anyway. There were twelve men here who were to
drive him out; and because I would not go alone, I took
Jeronimus with me. When we arrived, the floor of the
house was completely covered with tree bark over which
the devil-hunters were to walk. They were mostly old men
who were all colored or painted with red paint on their
faces because they were to perform something strange.
Three of them had garlands around their heads upon
which were five white crosses. These garlands were made
of deer's hair which they dyed with the roots of herbs. In
the middle of this house was a very sick person who had

been languishing for a long time, and there sat an old woman who had an empty turtle shell in her hands, in which were beads that rattled while she sang.[92] Here they intended to catch the devil and trample him to death, for they stomped all the bark in the house to pieces, so that none remained whole. Wherever they saw but a little dust on the corn, they beat at it with great excitement, and then they blew that dust toward one another and were so afraid that each did his best to flee as if he had seen the devil.[93] After much stomping and running, one of them went to the sick person and took an otter from his hand, and for a long time sucked on the sick man's neck and back. Then he spit in the otter and threw it on the ground, running away with great excitement. Other men then ran to the otter and performed such antics that it was a wonder to see; indeed, they threw fire, ate fire, and threw around hot ashes and embers in such a way that I ran out of the house.[94] Today I received another beaver.

Jan 5 I bought four dried salmon and two pieces of bear meat that was nine inches thick; there was some here even thicker. Today we ate beans cooked with bear meat. Otherwise nothing occurred.

Jan. 6. Nothing in particular happened other than I was shown some stones with which they make fire when they go into the woods, and which are scarce. These stones would also be good on firelocks.[95]

Jan. 7 We received a letter from Marten Gerritsz dated the last of December by a Sinck who came from our fort.[96] He said that our people were very troubled because we did not return, thinking that we had been killed. We ate here fresh salmon that had been caught but two days ago. 6-1/2 fathoms of sewant were stolen from our bags and never recovered.

Jan. 8 ARENIAS came to me and said that he would accompany me to our fort with all his pelts for trading. Jeronimus offered to sell his coat here but could not get rid of it.

Jan. 9 The Onnedagens[97] arrived here in the evening; 6 old men and 4 women, who were very tired from the journey. They brought some beaver pelts with them. I went and thanked them for coming to visit us. They welcomed me and because it was late I went again to our house.

Jan. 10 Jeronimus badly burned his pants that had fallen from his body into the fire during the night. The chief's mother gave him cloth to repair them and Willem Tomassen sewed them up again.

Jan. 11 The Indians came to me at 10 o'clock in the morning and said, "Come into the house where the Onnedagens sit in council and shall give you gifts." Jeronimus and I went there and took along a pistol. We sat down by an old man named CANASTOGEERA, who was about 55 years old.[98] He said to us, "Friends, I have come here to see you and to speak with you." We thanked him for this, and after they held council for a long time, an interpreter came to me and gave me 5 wild beavers for my journey and because we came to visit them. I took the beavers and thanked them, whereupon they shouted loudly 3 times NETHO, and then they laid another 5 wild beavers at my feet and gave them to us because we had come into his council house. We would have received many pelts as gifts, if we had just come into his country, and he asked me earnestly to visit his country in the summer. Then they gave me another 4 wild beavers and demanded that they must receive more for their pelts, then they would bring us many pelts. If I returned to their country in the summer, we would have 3 or 4 Indians to show us that lake and where the French came to trade with their sloops.[99] When we picked up our 14 beavers they shouted once again 3 times NETHO, and we fired 3 shots and gave the chiefs 2 pair of knives, some awls, and needles. Then we received the news that we could go. We still had 5 pieces of salmon and 2 pieces of bear meat to eat on the way, and we were given here some bread and meal to take along.

Jan. 12 We said goodbye, and when we thought that everything was ready, the Indians would not carry our goods—28 beavers and 5 salmon with some bread— because they all had enough to carry. However, after much grumbling and nice words, they went with us in company, carrying our goods. There were many people here who walked along with us shouting ALLE SARONDADE, that is to say, "Shoot!" When we passed the chief's grave, we fired 3 shots, and then they left us and went away. It was about 9 o'clock when we left here. We walked only about 5 miles through 2 1/2 feet of snow. It was very difficult going so that some Indians had to sleep in the woods in the snow, but we found a hut, where we slept.

Jan. 13 Early next morning we were once again on our way. After going another 7 or 8 miles, we came to a hut where we stopped to cook something to eat, and to sleep. ARENIAS pointed out to me a place on a high hill

and said that after a 10 days' journey we could come to
a river there where many people lived and where there
were many cows and horses. However, we must sail across
the river for a whole day and then travel another 6 days
to get there.[100] This was the place we passed on the 29th
of December. He did us much good.

Jan. 14 On Sunday we were ready to go, but the chief
wanted to stay in order to go out bear hunting from here.
However, because it was nice weather, I went on alone with
2 or 3 Indians. 2 Maquaesen came to us here because they
wanted to go to trade elk skins and SATTEEU.[101]

Jan. 15 In the morning 2 hours before daybreak, after
having eaten with the Indians, I continued my journey.
When it was almost dark, the Indians built a fire in the
woods, for they would go no farther. About 3 hours into evening I came to a hut where I had slept on December 26th.
It was very cold and I was not able to start a fire. Therefore
I had to walk around the whole night to keep warm.

Jan. 16 In the morning 3 hours before daybreak,
when the moon came up, I looked for the path, which
I finally found. At 9 in the morning after hard going, I
came to a great flat country. After traversing a high hill
I came upon a very level path which was made by the
Indians who had passed here with much venison when
returning home from the hunt to their castles. I saw the
castle at 10 o'clock and entered it at 12 noon. At least 100
people accompanied me in and showed me a house where
I was to stay. They gave me a white hare to eat, which they
had caught 2 days ago.[102] It was cooked with chestnuts.
I received a piece of wheat bread from an Indian who
had come from Fort Orange on the 15th of this month.

Toward evening about 40 fathoms of sewant were distributed among them as testimony for the Indians who had
died of the smallpox; this in the presence of the chiefs
and nearest friends, because it is their custom that they
distribute it thus to the chiefs and nearest friends. Toward
evening the Indians gave me 2 bear skins with which to
cover myself, and they fetched reeds to put under me. I
was also told that our people longed for our return.

Jan. 17 Jeronimus and Willem Tomassen arrived at
the castle TENOTOGEHAGE[103] with some other Indians.
They were still alert and healthy. In the evening another
100 fathoms of sewant were distributed to the chiefs and
friends of closest blood.

Jan. 18 We went again to this castle, that is to say, from
this castle to hasten our progress homeward. Although
there were in some houses here at least 40 or 50 quarters
of venison, cut and dried, they offered us little of it to
eat. After proceeding 1/2 mile, we passed through the village called KAWAOGE;[104] and 1/2 mile further we came to
the village Of OSQUAGO.[105] The chief OSQUAHOO[106]
received us well. We waited here for the chief AROMYAS,[107]
whom we had left in the castle Of TENOTOOGE.

Jan. 19 In the morning we continued our journey with
all haste. After traveling 1/2 mile we came to the third castle, called SCHANADISSE.[108] I looked into some houses
to see whether there were any pelts. I found 9 ONNED-
AGES there with pelts, whom I asked to accompany me to
the 2nd castle. The chief TATUROT was at home, that is
to say, TONEWEROT was at home, who pronounced us
welcome at once and gave us a very fat quarter of venison,
which we cooked.[109] As we were sitting eating, we received

a letter from Marten Gerrtsen by an Indian who was looking for us. It was dated the 8th of this month. We decided unanimously to proceed to the first castle as quickly as possible in order to depart for Fort Orange in the morning. We arrived at the first castle while the sun was still 3 hours high. We had bread baked here and packed the 3 other beavers that we had received from the chief when we first came here. We ate and slept here this night.

Jan. 20 In the morning before daybreak, Jeronimus sold his coat to an old man for 4 beavers. We left this place one hour before dawn. When we had covered about 2 miles, the Indians pointed to a high hill where their castle had stood 9 years ago, when they were driven out by the Mahicans.[110] Since that time they had not wanted to live there any longer. After traveling 7 or 8 miles, we found that the hunter's cabin had been burned so that we had to spend the night under the stars.

Jan. 21 Early in the morning we started out once again. After traveling for some time, we came upon a wrong path that was the most traveled, but because the Indians knew the paths better than we, they went back with us. After going 11 miles we came, praise and thank God, to Fort Orange the 21st of January Anno 1635.

NOTES

1. The term Maquasen, commonly Maquas, is a Dutch reference to the Mohawks, the easternmost of the five Iroquois nations, viz., from east to west, the Mohawks, the Oneidas, the Onondagas, the Cayugas, and then the Senecas. Various forms appear in seventeenth century

documents: Johan DeLaet recorded "Mackwaes" in 1625; in 1628 Jonas Michaelius has "Maechibaeys"; and in 1644, Johannes Megapolensis wrote "Mahakimbas" (see Jameson, ed., *Narratives*, 47, 131, 172). In 1634, the patroon Kiliaen van Rensselaer provided "Maquaes" (Van Laer, trans. and ed., *Van Rensselaer Bowier Manuscripts*, 306). "The most etymologically correct early spelling is Mohowawogs, 1638 (Roger Williams), which has the English plural -s added to a Narrangansett or Massachusett word for 'man-eaters', cognate with Unami *mhuwé·yɔk* 'cannibal monsters'." The Mohawks, however, then and now, refer to themselves as *kaynvʔkehró:nu* or *kanvyʔkehá:ka*, 'the flint people' or 'people of the place of the flint'. See Goddard's synonymy in Fenton and Tooker, "Mohawk," 478–79.

Through much of the seventeenth century, the Dutch applied the etymologically obscure term "Sinnekens" (various forms) to the Oneidas. Yet, on occasion, "Sinnekens" was used in reference to the Onondagas, and at times as a collective for any or all of the Iroquois living west of the Mohawks. Only later was the term restricted to the westernmost nation, the Senecas. See Goddard's synonymy in Abler and Tooker, "Seneca," 515–16.

Note: Unless otherwise indicated, all of the native language words and phrases recorded by Van den Bogaert are in Mohawk, with the possible exception of what he may have heard while he was at Oneida between December 30 and January 12. There, among a string of words, he wrote schenehalaton, which contains an Oneida "l." If this had been a Mohawk word, "r" would take the place of "l" (see note 91).

2. The commissary (Dutch *commies*) was responsible for managing the stores at West India Company trading posts, such as Fort Orange, as well as being commander of the garrison.

3. "French Indians" were natives allied to or in a trading relationship with the French. They included Algonquian- and Iroquoian-speaking peoples in southeastern Canada and northern New England.

4. A reference to authorities in the Netherlands, here either the directors of the West India Company or the States General.

5. The route taken by Van den Bogaert and his companions into the Mohawk Valley has often been described (Frey, "Notes";

Beauchamp, *Aboriginal Occupation*; Reid, *Mohawk Valley*; Ruttenber, *Footprints*; Greene, *Mohawk Valley*; Lathers and Sheehan, "Iroquois Occupation"; Clarke, *Bloody Mohawk*; Carse, "Mohawk Iroquois"; Grassmann, *Mohawk Indians*). In all cases there are problems in the interpretation of information from the journal, which lead to inaccuracies in distance and place (see Map).

Leaving Fort Orange with his Mohawk guides, Van den Bogaert reports that their direction was toward the northwest. This would have sent them across an expanse of flood and sand plains dominated by white pine, pitch pine, and oak forests—today's "Pine Bush"—lying between Albany and Schenectady. Note 15 provides a detailed discussion of the first part of the journey.

6. Van den Bogaert's unit of measure for distances traveled is *mylen* (miles), approximating 2.8 statute miles. However, current archaeological information on the locations of Mohawk villages encountered by the Dutchmen, in addition to details on the geography of the valley, render Van den Bogaert's estimates off the mark.

7. Oÿoge, *ohiò:ke* 'on the river', is not found in modern Mohawk. In 1646, "Oiogué" was recorded as an Iroquois name for the Hudson River (Thwaites, ed., *Jesuit Relations*, 29:49).

The directional preposition "into" used by Van den Bogaert is incorrect. From his vantage, the Mohawk River would flow "out of" the Mohawks' country. A similar confusion is mentioned in note 66.

8. The term "castle" denotes a large village (see note 14).

9. "The tributary" is the Mohawk River; "our river" is the Hudson. On December 11, the Dutchmen and their Mohawk guides approached the Mohawk River, found it in high flood, and unable or not choosing to cross, spent the night. Early the next day they proceeded generally west along the river, but not in view of it, and again made an approach, this time at a place where they could cross safely.

10. The typical watercraft of the Iroquois was not the light and sleek birch bark vessel used by native groups far to their north. Instead, these Indians traveled waterways in dugouts made of white pine, chestnut, and other woods, or in canoes constructed of tree bark, presumably from the once numerous American elm (Jameson, ed.,

Narratives, 176). Both were rather clumsy and unwieldy craft carrying just a few persons, although large dugouts are known from the lower Hudson Valley and southern New England. For early descriptions of Iroquois canoes and their methods of manufacture, see Lafitau, *Customs,* 1:124–26, and Benson, rev. and ed., *Peter Kalm's Travels,* 363. For additional information see Fenton and Dodge, "Elm Bark Canoe," and Adney and Chappelle, *Bark Canoes,* 213–19.

11. Van den Bogaert's party probably crossed to the north side of the Mohawk River somewhere in the vicinity of the cluster of islands close by present-day Schenectady and Scotia. This is clearly the most direct route between Fort Orange and Mohawk country. Also, the Mohawk River swings north here, and it is reasonable to assume that given their destination, they would have avoided going any farther off the trail than necessary (see Map for geographic points noted in Van den Bogaert's journal).

In 1642, Arent van Curler traveled into the valley in hopes of securing the release of the Jesuit father Isaac Jogues and his companions, held captive by the Mohawks. On his return, Van Curler commented on "the most beautiful land that eye may wish to see" adjacent to the Mohawk River "a full day's journey long and mostly in one unbroken piece" (Van Laer, "Arent van Curler," 28). In 1661, he and several others purchased a portion of this tract, the Great Flats, from the Mohawks and founded the settlement of Schenectady, a name derived from the Mohawk *skahnéhtati* 'it is beyond the pines' (Trelease, *Indian Affairs,* 136; Burke, *Mohawk Frontier,* 19–20). It is likely that Van Curler took the same path that Van den Bogaert had, one that led in a northwest direction from Fort Orange.

12. Van den Bogaert's descriptions of corn bread and other foods conform to those found in early firsthand accounts, some of which are prepared by Iroquois people today (see Parker, *Iroquois Uses of Maize*; Waugh, *Iroquois Foods*).

13. Van den Bogaert's observation that there were many islands in this stretch of the river securely establishes that the party had initially crossed the Mohawk in the vicinity of Schenectady and Scotia. Prior to the construction of the Erie Canal, begun in the first decades of the

nineteenth century, and then the New York State Barge Canal, completed in 1918, there were nearly a score of islands in the river from this point to about the mouth of Schoharie Creek. From the Schoharie west, no islands would have been encountered until about six miles upriver from Fonda, above the "Noses" at Yosts and beyond where the Dutchmen recrossed the river to the south side (Wright, "Mohawk River"; Hutchinson, "Maps"; O'Callaghan, ed., *Documentary History*, 3:659–70). A *morgen* is a Dutch land measurement equivalent to just over two acres (Van Laer, trans. and ed., *Van Rensselaer Bowier Manuscripts*, 847).

14. Castle (Dutch, *casteel*). Van den Bogaert, and other Dutch, sometimes intimated a distinction between settlement types, the castle and the village. "Castles" were commonly large, heavily palisaded towns, thus corresponding to the European experience. "Village" was used for smaller settlements whose residents, it is believed, moved to the fortified and more secure castles in times of danger (Abler, "Longhouse and Palisade," 25–28). On other occasions these terms were used interchangeably. For some Europeans, "castle" denoted one or more of the Iroquois nations: that is, a political entity.

15. The locations of the Mohawk villages visited by Van den Bogaert have been searched for since the journal's initial publication. The resulting narratives offer different scenarios in which, in each case, the distances Van den Bogaert estimated between settlements were marked off and correlated with the physiographic details he provided for each locale—for example, situated on a "high hill" or near a "big stream." This information was then compared to what was then known of the historical and archaeological data. However, the conclusions drawn in these various accounts have proven to be less than satisfactory.

Reid, *Mohawk Valley*, working from questionable sources and with little critical insight, incorrectly places the first settlement, Onekahoncka (see note 28), near present-day Mariaville, and the second castle, Canagere (see note 32), east of Schoharie Creek, far from their probable locations. A less than careful reading of the journal by Greene, *Mohawk Valley*, and his reliance on the work of a local antiquarian, a Mr. Fea, caused him to place one village at the site of the former Montgomery County Home, north of the river and west of Fonda.

He leaves the remaining villages on the south side of the river. Clarke, *Bloody Mohawk*, using Greene as a source for his own work, also puts one village on the north side of the Mohawk, this in spite of the fact that Van den Bogaert has all of the villages south of the river. Finally, Carse, "Mohawk Iroquois," 7, writes that "at the time of Van Corlear's [read Van den Bogaert's] journey in 1634, probably all of the Mohawk 'castles' were east of the modern city of Canajoharie," an obvious error.

Other than demonstrating where previous writers stumbled in their identification of village sites, our new translation still does not provide for the precise locations of the settlements visited by Van den Bogaert. However, a long-term archaeological research project, plans for which were formulated by Dean Snow and William Starna in 1980–81, with field excavations initiated in 1982 and continued by Snow from 1984 until their completion in 1991, offers solutions to what has previously been a confusing situation (see Snow, *Mohawk Valley Archaeology*).

In the journal, Van den Bogaert's party crossed on foot to the south side of the river, which had frozen over during the night. It is likely that the river was relatively deep and slow moving at this point, allowing for a surface freeze solid enough to permit a safe passage, a phenomenon that was observed by Warren Johnson, Sir William Johnson's brother, in December 1760 (Snow, Gehring, and Starna, eds., *Mohawk Country*, 260). A report dated 1792 details a survey of the Mohawk River made prior to canalization. It describes a rift at Caughnawaga, a locale west of Fonda. From the mouth of Schoharie Creek to this rift, a distance of about six miles, the river is said to have been "very good water, deep and gently [*sic*]." Both above and below this stretch were rapids and rifts, a less than favorable condition for water or ice floes to freeze rapidly: that is, overnight (O'Callaghan, ed., *Documentary History*, 3:659–70). Ruttenber (*Footprints*, 196) maintained that the rapids and rifts just east of the mouth of Schoharie Creek were never known to have frozen in such a short period of time. Thus, it is likely that the party crossed over the river to what was the first castle a short distance west of the Schoharie, a waterway that was not encountered directly by the Dutchmen.

Van den Bogaert states that on December 12 they left a hunter's cabin in the Pine Bush three hours before dawn. The winter sun would have risen at c. 7:15 A.M. on that day, putting their departure at about 4:15 A.M. They traveled one hour (c. 5:15 A.M.), and crossed the Mohawk River to the north bank (an estimated one-half hour to accomplish this, resuming their trek at c. 5:45 A.M.). They traveled a distance, stopping at another hunter's cabin where they ate (spending an estimated one-half hour) and then resumed their journey. At one hour into the evening (c. 5:20 P.M., as evening for the Dutch began at sunset, which took place at c. 4:20 P.M. that day) they stopped at a cabin one-half mile from the first castle.

The total time the party spent on the trail was between eleven and twelve hours. Assuming a walking speed of two miles per hour, a reasonable rate considering the conditions, they would have traveled some twenty-two to twenty-four miles generally west from the spot where they had first crossed the Mohawk River. The Dutchmen do not appear to have passed beyond Fonda, and most likely crossed to the south bank at a point at or just east of this place. This is concluded from negative evidence: that is, there is no mention of the party having encountered Cayadutta Creek, a large tributary running south into the Mohawk River on the western edge of Fonda. In the journal, Van den Bogaert is careful to note the presence of large streams. Based on his consistency in this regard, if he had crossed the Cayadutta it is unlikely that he would have failed to mention it.

With the knowledge that the river was first crossed between Scotia and Schenectady, that the distance traveled along the north side was considerable, and that they recrossed the river over the ice to the first castle, in addition to a consideration of current archaeological information, it is possible to locate the position of the first settlement, Onekahoncka, in the town of Glen, Montgomery County, near the unincorporated hamlet of Stone Ridge (Snow, *Mohawk Valley Archaeology*, 281–82) (see Map for this and subsequent village locations).

16. The houses described by Van den Bogaert are typical of the "longhouses" of Northern Iroquoian people. Historical accounts, and more reliably, archaeological data, demonstrate that such houses

were generally twenty feet wide, with lengths varying from forty to more than 200 feet. The average Mohawk house was close to 140 feet long (Van den Bogaert estimated the lengths of the houses by simply stepping them off). Houses were constructed by first setting into the ground a series of poles fashioned from saplings several inches in diameter, following a rectangular floor plan. The poles formed straight outer walls rising to a height of about twelve feet to support an arched roof with a well-defined drip edge (see fig. 6). At the apex of the arched roofs, houses approached heights of fifteen feet. Once the entire framework was erected, it was covered with large shingles of elm bark, leaving an entrance at each end. Movable bark sheets at the open peak of the roof might be adjusted to provide for light and ventilation.

House interiors were divided into compartments along each side, measuring approximately twenty feet in length and seven feet deep. A central aisle ran the length of the house. Hearths, placed in the aisle, were shared by the occupants of opposing compartments. Each compartment housed a nuclear family, while the whole house was the residential unit for a household or a matrilineage, a kin group composed of people who traced their descent through related females. There was often a storage area at one or both ends of a longhouse, sometimes built as an extension on the house and covered with a shed roof. Additional storage space was available between compartments and in and around sleeping platforms constructed against the house wall. Covered with reed mats and furs, sleeping platforms were raised about a foot off the ground to avoid dampness, cold, and vermin. For authoritative discussions on the architecture of Iroquois longhouses, and Mohawk longhouses in particular, see Snow, *Iroquois,* 40–46, and Snow, "Iroquois Longhouses."

17. The presence of iron materials among the Mohawks is interesting, but not surprising. By 1580, and perhaps a few years before this date, European trade goods were being acquired by Mohawk raiding parties operating in the St. Lawrence Valley (Pendergast, "Introduction of European Goods"; Trigger, "Early Iroquoian Contacts"; Lenig, *Of Dutchmen,* 73). More direct availability followed the construction of Fort Nassau, a Dutch trading house near present-day Albany, in 1614.

By 1624, and following the abandonment of Fort Nassau several years earlier, Fort Orange provided the Mohawks with nearly all of the trade goods they desired. The materials that Van den Bogaert saw do not, for the most part, represent the normal fare of trade items. However, hinges, spikes, bolts, and the rest were either manufactured or could otherwise be found in Rensselaerswijck at about this time, and one way or another, were acquired by the Mohawks (Van Laer, trans. and ed., *Van Rensselaer Bowier Manuscripts,* 351; Bradley, *Evolution of the Onondaga Iroquois* and *Before Albany*).

18. Corn is *ó:nvhste?* in modern Mohawk and was the most important domesticated plant among the Iroquoians (see Parker, *Iroquois Uses of Maize*; Waugh, *Iroquois Foods*). Although there are no comparable figures for the Iroquois, Heidenreich (*Huronia,* 163) estimates that for each Huron person, approximately 65 percent of the daily caloric intake and 43 percent of the daily bulk intake was from corn. However, there may have been somewhat less of a reliance placed on this grain by the Iroquois, given their emphasis on hunting, which played a larger dietary role than for the Huron (Fenton, "Northern Iroquoian Culture Patterns," 298).

Skipple (Dutch, *schepel*). A Dutch dry measure equivalent to three-quarters of a bushel (Van Laer, trans. and ed., *Van Rensselaer Bowier Manuscripts,* 849).

19. The modern Mohawk equivalent is *onu?úsera?* 'squash'.

20. This man's name, or what Van den Bogaert may have been told this man was called, is *ateryóhtu* in modern Mohawk. It contains the verb *-ryoht-* 'to die from something', found for instance in *yakoryóhtha?* 'one dies from it' or 'poison'. One native speaker suggested that a close literal translation of Adriochten might be 'he has caused others to die'. This interpretation, when considered with the knowledge that this man lived one-quarter of a mile from his village because many of the Indians there had died from smallpox, implies that Adriochten was perhaps in some way blamed for the epidemic and had been subsequently banished. In this case, Adriochten could have been a nickname of sorts. Incidentally, Adriochten may be identical to Saggodryochta, a "head chief" of the Mohawks, who in 1633 had an unpleasant

encounter with one Hans Hontom, a violently disposed troublemaker, while trading pelts at Fort Orange. It was Hontom who in 1622 murdered another Mohawk chief, an act that neither Saggodryochta nor the Mohawks had forgotten (Van Laer, trans. and ed., *Van Rensselaer Bowier Manuscripts,* 303; Gehring and Starna, "Dutch and Indians," 14–16).

Like most other American Indians, the Mohawks suffered greatly from a series of epidemics that resulted from contact with Europeans. Introduced diseases such as smallpox, measles, typhus, and others were particularly devastating. Indian populations had no immunity to these Old World pathogens and went into rapid decline. The Mohawks were struck by a first epidemic in the third decade of the seventeenth century, although there may have been an earlier contagion. It was then that they found themselves in frequent and often prolonged contact with the Dutch citizens near Fort Orange. In addition, exposure to Algonquian groups in the Hudson Valley and parts of New England, who had suffered earlier epidemics, would have been a contributing factor (see Snow, *Iroquois* and "Mohawk Demography"; Snow and Lanphear, "European Contact"; Snow and Starna, "Sixteenth Century Depopulation"). For the most recent statement on a causative disease for the devastating 1616–19 epidemic in New England, leptospirosis complicated by Weil syndrome, see Marr and Cathey, "New Hypothesis."

21. Beaver pelts were the most valuable and ubiquitous commodity traded by Indians, and obviously, sought by Europeans.

22. The letter written by Jeronimus dela Croix does not survive, nor does his map (see entry of December 13). A manuscript and accompanying map, claimed to be by Dela Croix, allegedly discovered in a parcel of documents bequeathed to L. G. van Loon and subsequently translated and published by him, are fakes (see Van Loon, "Letter"; Gehring and Starna, "Case of Fraud").

According to Van den Bogaert, Dela Croix asked for not only salt and paper, but also tobacco, atsochwat. However, atsochwat does not mean Indian tobacco. It contains the verb root *-atshokw-* 'to have a smoke'. 'I smoke' is *katshókwas*. The modern Mohawk equivalent for tobacco is *oyú:kwaʔ*. Although Indians grew their own tobacco, Van den Bogaert wanted cut tobacco, available only from the stores at Fort Orange, for smoking in his and his companions' pipes. The request for salt, undoubtedly to be used as a condiment, suggests that it was not used for this purpose among the Mohawks. In fact, such practice is not reported for any of the Northern Iroquoians (Fenton, "Northern Iroquoian Culture Patterns," 298). Support for this observation is found in Thwaites, ed., *Jesuit Relations*, 6:267, 7:45, 18:17, and Sagard-Théodat, *Long Journey*, 80, 112. There appear conflicting statements regarding the use of salt as a preservative.

23. Sewant is from Pidgin Delaware "<seawan> 'wampum', presumably from a Northern Unami word for 'loose wampum'; cf. Munsee *sé·wan* 'it is scattered, all over the place'" (Goddard, "Linguistic Variation," 43n27). Sewant or wampum are cylindrical shell beads with a central aperture, strung on fiber cords or woven into belts. Early on, the beads were made from several species of marine shell, especially the whelk (*Buccinum undatum*), the source for white beads, and the hard-shelled clam (*Venus mercenaria*), the source for purple beads. True wampum, that is, cylindrical and not discoidal beads, first appears in Iroquois country in the sixteenth century, having been obtained through trade primarily with the Indians of southern New England, in particular the Pequots and Narragansetts. At this time it functioned in a ceremonial or political context. It was not at first used as currency, contrary to the popular image. However, following the establishment of Fort Orange in 1624, both the quantity and distribution of wampum increased, and it quickly became a medium of exchange. For discussions on the history, manufacture, and use of wampum see Fenton, "New York State Wampum Collection"; Ceci, "Effect of European Contact" and "Value of Wampum"; Tooker, "League of the Iroquois"; Peña, "Wampum Production"; McBride, "Eastern New Netherland"; and Bradley, *Before Albany* and "Revisting Wampum."

A "hand" is a common European linear measurement, equivalent to about four inches.

24. Corn, beans, and pumpkins (squashes), all mentioned several times in the journal, formed the triad of domesticated plants

that among contemporary Iroquois are known as "the three sisters" (Parker, *Iroquois Uses of Maize*; Waugh, *Iroquois Foods*; Fenton, "Northern Iroquoian Culture Patterns," 299). The earliest evidence for corn and squashes in the archaeological record has been dated from about C.E. 800 to C.E. 1000. Beans appear about C.E. 1300. Other plants cultivated by the Iroquois and other natives in the Northeast included sunflowers and tobacco. For an excellent discussion on Iroquois farming, see Engelbrecht, *Iroquoia*, 22–33.

25. Duffel, a thick-napped coarse woolen cloth, was an important and popular trade item.

26. Persons identified in the literature as "diviners," "clairvoyants," and "fortune tellers"—related kinds of ritual practitioners—along with their activities and paraphenalia, are described at length in Lafitau, *Customs*, 1:237–47; Tooker, *Huron Indians*, 83–87; and Trigger, *Children of Aataentsic*. Perspectives on these actors as they function in contemporary Iroquois communities are found in Shimony, *Conservatism among the Iroquois*; Fenton, *False Faces*; Fenton, *Little Water Medicine Society*; and Herrick, *Iroquois Medical Botany*.

The pigeon mentioned is either the passenger pigeon (*Ectopistes migratorius*, extinct), or the mourning dove (*Zenaida macroura*).

27. Sickaris in modern Mohawk is *shikká:rus* 'while I am peeling the bark off'. *Shi-* is a prepronominal prefix called the coincident, *-k-* is the pronoun 'I', *-kar-* is the verb root 'to peel bark off', and *-us* is the serial aspect suffix. A name of this grammatical form is rather uncommon.

The items mentioned are standard European trade goods made available to the Mohawks.

28. In the place-name Onekahoncka, the first settlement visited by Van den Bogaert and his companions, native speakers recognized only the noun root *-hnek-* 'water' or 'liquid', and could provide no further information on its meaning.

29. This word in modern Mohawk is *kanú:warote?* 'a nail stuck into the wall'. It consists of the noun root *-nuwar-* 'nail', and the verb root *-ot-* 'to be standing'. This village was located in the vicinity of Randall, town of Root, Montgomery County (Snow, *Mohawk Valley Archaeology*, 280).

30. Schatsyerosy was apparently without a palisade. This word looks like *skatsi?eróhtsyu* 'one fingernail removed' and contains the noun root *-tsi?er-* and the verb root *-ohtsy-* 'to remove'. This settlement was also in the town of Root, off Currytown Road, overlooking Yatesville Creek (Snow, *Mohawk Valley Archaeology,* 304).

31. Mohawk cemeteries, often two or three in number, were usually placed close to the village (see note 70).

32. This village, identified as the second castle by Van den Bogaert, is nonetheless without a palisade. It was located just south of Sprakers (Snow, *Mohawk Valley Archaeology,* 309–10). This word may be *kaná:kare?* 'sticks'. On palisades, see note 53.

33. This and the sentence that follows indicate that here, as well as in Onekahoncka, the inhabitants had gone hunting, an activity in which both men and women participated (Trigger, *Children of Aataentsic,* 1:39; Fenton, "Northern Iroquoian Culture Patterns," 298).

34. Tonnosatton, which contains the noun root *-nuhs-* 'house' and the verb root *-ahtu-* 'to disappear', could be *thonuhsáhtu* 'he takes the whole house away'. Toniwerot may contain the noun root *-wer-* 'wind' or 'air'.

35. The original document reads *met sij eygen honden,* that is, 'with his own dogs'. Although on December 12 there is a reference to dogs, it is doubtful that they would have been used to hunt beavers. Writing of the Huron in 1632, the Recollect lay brother Gabriel Sagard-Théodat (*Long Journey,* 233–34) observed that in summer, beavers were taken with nets stretched over poles. In winter, he maintained, a hole was made through the ice near the beaver's house and men reached in and grabbed the animal by its scruff as it tried to escape. In the face of this rather implausible tale, it is our position that *honden* is a copyist's error for *handen* 'hands'. Thus, in winter, as in other seasons, beavers were probably snared or otherwise trapped by native hunters, that is, through the use of "his own hands." Beavers were not only exploited for their valuable pelts, but at the same time, they were a source of food, increasing in importance as trade and the demand for pelts intensified (see Grayson, "Riverhaven No. 2"; Lenig, *Of Dutchmen,* 73).

36. The keeping of bears in enclosures within a village seems to have been a relatively uncommon practice among Northern

Iroquoians. Tooker (*Huron Indians*, 66) and Heidenreich (*Huronia*, 202, 204–5) summarize observations by Champlain and Sagard, noting that bears, probably cubs whose mothers had been killed, might be fattened for two or three years and then butchered and eaten in celebration of a feast (Trigger, *Children of Aataentsic*, 1:41). The structures in which they were penned were, as Van den Bogaert describes, small log houses or round cage-like enclosures formed by driving stakes into the ground. Sagard-Théodat (*Long Journey*, 220) says that the bears were fed *sagamité*—boiled corn soup—, while Van den Bogaert remarks that the one he saw "ate everything given to it" (see note 64). Bears were and are considered important animals to the Iroquois. Once a source of food and fur, they today retain a prominent position in Iroquois ideology and ceremony. The Bear Society is one of a number of medicine societies in Iroquois communities and the Bear dance an integral part of the Midwinter Ceremony (see Tooker, *Huron Indians*; Tooker, *Iroquois Ceremonial of Midwinter*; Fenton, *False Faces*; Shimony, *Conservatism among the Iroquois*, 173–91).

37. The source of the sulfur (S. Orthorhombic) mentioned by Van den Bogaert was probably the Silurian evaporate beds located in the Buffalo-Rochester region of the state, where deposits of the Salina group—dolomite, halite, and anhydrite—produce this substance (Robert Dineen and Richard Wiener, Geological Survey, New York State Museum and Science Service, personal communication, 1980). The Mohawks told Van den Bogaert that they had acquired the sulfur from "foreign Indians," perhaps in trade with the Eries, the Wenros, or the Neutrals, Iroquoian speakers then resident in western New York and southern Ontario (see White, "Neutral and Wenro" and "Erie"). The Indians may have used sulfur as a fumigant or in medicines.

38. Guilder, a Dutch monetary unit. In the Netherlands during the first half of the seventeenth century, a guilder constituted a day's wage for a common laborer.

The presence of women on the trail without the escort of men and transporting items to trade is of some interest. Although it has been suggested that trade was fundamentally a male activity, women may have played an increasingly important role following a general population decline and male deaths as a result of epidemics and warfare, but also in response to the presence of Europeans and the associated availability of trade goods (Tooker, *Huron Indians,* 58; Trigger, *Children of Aataentsic,* 1:62–65; Engelbrecht, "Iroquois Pottery Decoration," 8; cf. Waterman, trans. and ed., *To Do Justice,* 17–18). However, perhaps women had always been involved at some level in trade and their participation has simply gone unreported. Identified as "sinnekens," these women were in all likelihood Oneidas. The native Atlantic salmon (*Salmo salar*) then ascended, as it does now, the Oswego and Oneida Rivers and other tributaries to Lake Ontario and the St. Lawrence River. This fish was not present in the Mohawk River.

39. This letter has not been located.

40. Squohea may be the Mohawk noun *oskóhara?* 'skeleton'.

41. Moving west from the fourth village, the only major stream encountered matching the description offered here is Canajoharie Creek.

42. The location of this fifth settlement, "the third castle," is in the town of Canajoharie, Montgomery County, off Happy Hollow Road about midway between the villages of Canajoharie and Fort Plain (Snow, *Mohawk Valley Archaeology,* 289). Schanidisse resembles *skanatísu?* 'the town has been remade'. This could be segmented as *s-* 'again', *-ka-* 'it', *-nat-* 'town', *-is-* 'to complete, finish', and *-u,* a stative suffix. It may be that Schanidisse had only recently been built and that Van den Bogaert's query about what the village was called was misdirected by him or misunderstood by the Indians, so that he received the answer "the town has been remade."

Tewowary is possibly *tehóhare?* 'he has suspended something in two different places'. This word contains the dualic prefix *te-,* the pronoun *-h-* 'he', the verb root *-ohar-* 'to suspend something', and the stative suffix *-e?*.

43. The skin may have been that of a mountain lion or eastern cougar (*Felis concolor cougar*), today believed extirpated from the region, or alternatively, and perhaps more likely, a lynx or bobcat.

44. This village was on Prospect Hill in Fort Plain (Snow, *Mohawk Valley Archaeology,* 301–4). Osquage is probably *ohskwà:ke,* which is *ahskwà:ke* in modern Mohawk. This word means 'on top of the roof'. Native

speakers pointed out that this kind of roof has no walls but only posts. Oquoho is *okwáho* 'wolf', used either in connection with the animal or with a member of the Wolf Clan. Native speakers insisted that it cannot be used as a personal name. Thus, it appears that Van den Bogaert had been told of this chief's clan affiliation, that is, he is a member of the Wolf Clan, he is a Wolf. There are three clans among the Mohawks: the Turtle Clan, the Bear Clan, and the Wolf Clan. Composed of multiple lineages of related women (matrilineages), clans function primarily as fictive kin groups and in ceremonial contexts.

45. This is Otsquago Creek at Fort Plain.

46. Minquas, a Dutch reference to the Susquehannock Indians (see Jennings, "Susquehannock").

47. A brief mention in Lafitau, *Customs,* 1:215, supports the supposition that additional individuals might be called in to assist ill persons if curing them was considered hopeless or interest in effecting a cure had diminished.

48. Cawaoge could be *kahahò:ke* 'a place where the road is submerged'. This word contains the neuter pronoun *ka-* 'it', the noun root *-hah-* 'road', the verb root *-o-* 'be in the water', and the locative suffix *-ke*. The site of this village, largely destroyed by highway construction and gravel mining, was a short distance northwest of Fort Plain (Snow, *Mohawk Valley Archaeology,* 325).

49. Van den Bogaert's savin, also savin juniper (*Juniperus sabina*), is a Eurasian native. A physically similar species in North America is the common juniper (*Juniperus communis* L.). More widespread, although much larger, is the eastern red cedar (*Juniperus virginica*).

50. Tenotoge is *teyonutó:kv* 'between two mountains' or 'valley'. It contains the dualic prefix *te-*, the neuter pronoun *-yo-* 'it', the noun root *-nut-* 'mountain', and the verb root *-okv* 'two things forking or merging'. The eighth village visited by Van den Bogaert, Tenotoge was on a very large hill some one and one-third miles northwest of Fort Plain. The site was destroyed by the construction of the New York State Thruway in the early 1950s (Snow, *Mohawk Valley Archaeology,* 294).

51. Evidence of structures, perhaps those used for the storage of corn, as Van den Bogaert observed, has been discovered near the

mouth of Caroga Creek, a tributary on the north side of the Mohawk River (Donald Lenig, personal communication, 1976).

52. Unlike Canagere, this village is fully populated. It is likely that the residents of each village hunted at different times during the winter so that one village might have been nearly abandoned, its population dispersed in hunting parties, while at another, people might have been at home. It is also possible that the residents of Tenotoge had very recently returned from the winter hunt.

53. The deteriorated condition of what had been a triple palisade around this village suggests that it had been occupied for many years. A move to a new village may have been imminent. See Starna, Hamell, and Butts, "Northern Iroquoian Horticulture," for a detailed discussion of the reasons behind village relocations.

The forms and techniques of palisade construction among Northern Iroquoians are discussed in Engelbrecht, *Iroquoia,* 96–99 and passim. Generally, two or three rows of posts or timbers were driven into the ground encircling a village. The outer and inner rows were angled toward each other and secured at the top. Sheets of bark and saplings were interwoven or otherwise secured among the uprights, reinforcing them and forming a virtually impenetrable wall twelve to twenty or more feet in height. Platforms or galleries on which warriors could position themselves were often built near the top of the wall.

54. This description of Mohawk armament and armor corresponds well with that of other Iroquoian groups where twined reed armor or a cuirass covering the chest, arms, and legs, along with a skin shield and leather cap, were worn. Weapons included the bow and arrow and ball-headed war clubs (Tooker, *Huron Indians,* 30; Trigger, *Children of Aataentsic,* 1:70, 196–97, 252; Lafitau, *Customs,* 1:115–16, plate VIII; Fenton, "Northern Iroquoian Culture Patterns," 316). Note the absence of guns (see note 56).

55. For a history of scalping and other forms of procuring war trophies, see Axtell and Sturtevant, "Who Invented Scalping." Killing and scalping were not the prime directives of Iroquoian warfare. Instead, the preferred alternative was to take their enemies captive—men, women, and children—and return with them to their home villages.

There the prisoners would be made slaves, an act that has often been interpreted by scholars as exclusively a form of adoption. If the prisoners resisted or proved intractable, or as in the case of captured warriors, were considered dangerous and thus a threat to the community, they faced torture and death (see Starna and Watkins, "Northern Iroquoian Slavery"; Richter, "War and Culture"; Richter, *Ordeal of the Longhouse*, 32–38, 65–74; Brandão, *Your fyre shall burn no more*).

56. This is the first of four instances where the Dutchmen are asked to fire their weapons, in all likelihood wheel lock holster pistols. The obvious curiosity of the Mohawks expressed here and elsewhere in the journal clearly indicates that they had not yet acquired firearms, which remained the case until about 1640 (Fenton, "Northern Iroquoian Culture Patterns," 316; Richter, *Ordeal of the Longhouse*, 62–64 and passim; Hunt, *Wars of the Iroquois*, 166–69). However, by 1642 the situation had so changed that, as Arent van Curler reported it, his party was "obliged to halt fully a quarter of an hour before each [Mohawk] castle, in order that the Indians might salute us by the firing of muskets" (Van Laer, "Arent van Curler," 28).

57. The appearance in June of wild strawberries (*Fragaria vesca americana* and *Fragaria virginiana*) is celebrated in the annual Strawberry Ceremony. Today, and in the recent past, its purpose is to give thanks for the first fruits of the new season and to entertain the food spirits to insure continued good harvests (see Shimony, *Conservatism among the Iroquois*, 158–61; Morgan, *League of the Iroquois*, 197–98).

58. Chestnuts, from the American chestnut (*Castanea dentata*), since devastated in its historic range by a fungal blight that began in New York City in 1904; blueberries (*Vaccinium*), eight native species; and sunflower seeds from the sunflower plant (*Helianthus*), of which there are six native species, including the tuberous Jerusalem artichoke (Starna, "Checklist of Higher Edible Plants").

59. Van den Bogaert's wordlist (see Wordlist) contains sinachkoo, with the given meaning "(to) exorcise the devil." The modern form *hatsináhkv* 'exorcist' was known to one informant in Kahnawake, who said that it was used on the Six Nations Reserve in Ontario. The Jesuit missionary Jacques Bruyas, who did his linguistic fieldwork in Mohawk

country in the 1670s, also came across this term, which he recorded as *Atsinnachen 'jongleur'* (Bruyas, "Radical Words," 43). In his observations on what are best described as ritual practitioners, Lafitau (*Customs*, 1:237) provides the word *agotsinnachen* 'seers'. All of these Mohawk forms contain the verb root *-tsin-* 'to be energetic', perhaps suggesting the exercises or exertions of such persons in the performance of their duties. On sticks inserted into throats, see Lafitau, *Customs*, 1:244.

60. An ell is a standard of measurement equal to 27 inches.

61. The curing rituals described by Van den Bogaert (see also entry for January 4) are some of the most detailed found in the literature. Refer to discussions on illness, medicine, herbalism, shamanism, and curing in Fenton, *False Faces*; Fenton, *Little Water Medicine Society*; Shimony, *Conservatism among the Iroquois*; Tooker, *Huron Indians*; Herrick, *Iroquois Medical Botany*); Trigger, *Children of Aataentsic*; and Lafitau, *Customs*, 1.

62. Again, the Mohawks ask the Dutchmen to fire their weapons. Allese rondade or alle sarondade (see entry of January 12) is *á:re sarú:tat* 'fire again!' in modern Mohawk. *á:re* means 'again', and the verb root *-aruʔtat-* means 'to blow' or 'to shoot'. Compare *arontaton 'souffler'* (Bruyas, "Radical Words," 26).

63. Elk (*Cervus canadensis*) were once found in the region.

64. This a variant form of *samp* (Narragansett *nasaump*), meaning corn soup or mush. The French called this food *sagamité* (Waugh, *Iroquois Foods*, 91–93).

65. After leaving Tenotoge, Van den Bogaert and his companions appear to have traveled overland in a nearly westerly direction. There is no evidence in the journal to suggest that they continued to follow the Mohawk River. Instead, they probably passed south of the river in as direct a route as possible to the Oneida village. Van den Bogaert's observations of going "over hills and through thickets" as the party hiked through forests of oak, birch, and beech lend support to this view. Their destination was the country of the Onneyuttehage, the Oneidas (see note 82). Several Oneida villages, all of which cluster in the southeast section of present-day Madison County, have been identified archaeologically (Pratt, *Oneida Iroquois*, 171, fig. 5).

66. The streams that Van den Bogaert and his party crossed are not easily identified. That they "flowed" in the direction he describes may be an error or a misunderstanding of his Indian guides (note 7 makes reference to Van den Bogaert's difficulties with directional prepositions). That is, if these streams were tributaries of the Mohawk, they would have flowed *north*. The Indians may have said, for example, that following the streams south would eventually lead him to that river which flowed into the Minquas's country, the Susquehanna, or to the Delaware, called by the Dutch the South River. On the other hand, since his route to the Oneidas may have run along the divide between the Mohawk and Susquehanna watersheds, it is possible that he crossed the headwaters of several south-flowing waterways: North Winfield Creek and the West Branch of the Unadilla.

67. River otter (*Lutra canadensis*).

68. Van den Bogaert's generic "ironwood" was either the Eastern hophornbeam (*Carpinus caroliniana*) or the American hornbeam (*Ostrya virginiana*).

69. From a high vantage near the Oneida village, the Indians are pointing out to Van den Bogaert the Mohawk River. Their location at this time was probably on one of several high hills some twenty miles south of the river, where such a view would have been possible. On the previous day (December 29), Van den Bogaert writes of coming to "a very high hill."

70. Van den Bogaert's observations agree with other descriptions of graves and burial practices among Northern Iroquoians found in Lafitau, *Customs,* 2:231–35; Tooker, *Huron Indians,* 130; Trigger, *Children of Aataentsic,* 1:52–53; and others. See also Van der Donck, *Description of New Netherland,* 88–90. The body of a deceased person was placed in a flexed position, with the legs drawn up to the chest and the arms arranged so that the hands were near or over the face. Wrapped tightly in furs or hides, a robe, or other clothing, the corpse was laid in a grave lined with bark or woven mats. Goods such as food, weapons, tools, and personal items were included to accompany the spirit of the deceased on its final journey.

71. The high ground mentioned is the escarpment of the Tug Hill Plateau, which begins north of Boonville.

72. This is a reference to Oneida Lake, about eighteen to twenty miles north-northwest from the Oneida village. The French entered the lake via the Oswego and Oneida Rivers.

73. The greeting given Van den Bogaert and his party followed Iroquois custom, although similar forms were practiced by many other native peoples in the Northeast, as attested by the numerous reports of first-hand observers.

74. Pratt (*Oneida Iroquois*, 136), following Whitney ("Thurston"), has suggested that the Oneida village Van den Bogaert arrived at is today the Thurston site, town of Stockbridge, Madison County. However, there are several other archaeological sites in the Oneida sequence that fall within the time frame of the first half of the seventeenth century, making each of them candidates for the village Van den Bogaert visited.

75. There are few references to or descriptions of the aesthetic, decorative, or symbolic elements or motifs that might be found on or inside of Iroquois longhouses. Lafitau (*Customs*, 2:20) mentions that houses were decorated on the inside, while Morgan (*League of the Iroquois*, 318) says that over one of the usual two entrances to a longhouse was "cut the tribal device of the head of the family." Van den Bogaert may have seen gables painted with animal figures depicting the clan of the women of the household. Among the Oneidas, as was the case with the Mohawks, there were and are three clans: the Turtle, the Bear, and the Wolf.

76. The councillor referred to was a village chief or headman.

77. Van den Bogaert is being chastised for not having participated in a protocol fundamental not only to the Iroquois, but to other cultures as well. This is reciprocity, an underlying principle governing social interaction where obligations are incurred and met, often taking the form of gift giving or gift exchange. Conventions such as these functioned to forge and maintain social, political, and economic alliances and networks.

78. The river is the Oswego or the Oneida, connecting Lake Ontario and Oneida Lake.

79. Salmon and other fish were taken in a number of ways by Northern Iroquoians, including the use of weirs, gill nets, seines, and spears. Although fish were obviously available throughout the year, the peak fishing season was March through May, when large numbers of fish ascended rivers and their tributaries to spawn. Waugh (*Iroquois Foods*, 136) briefly discusses fish as a food resource among the Iroquois. On comparative Huron fishing practices, see Heidenreich, *Huronia*, 208–12.

80. Jawe is *nyá:wv* 'thank you'. Arenias, one informant suggested, could be analyzed as *arénye?s* 'he spreads himself', 'he is a charismatic person', with *-areny-* 'to spread', and the habitual suffix *-e?s*.

81. It is unlikely that there were people with horns living in the Tug Hill Plateau region at this or any other time. By making such a claim, however, the Indians were doubtlessly attempting to discourage the Dutchmen from exploring the region, and, which would be to their disadvantage, expanding the trade. The Indians may also have feared that a Dutch presence there would disrupt their own trade with the French.

82. Onneyuttehage is *Onvyote?á:ka* 'the people of the standing stone', that is, the Oneidas, Iroquoian-speakers located immediately west of the Mohawks (see Campisi, "Oneida"). This Mohawk-language term consists of the noun prefix *o-* 'it', the noun root *-nvy-* 'stone', the verb root *-ot-* 'to be standing', the aspect suffix *-e?-*, and the populative *-(h)aka* 'people'.

83. In old Huron "*Ho, ho, ho*" was a "salutation of joy" (Sagard-Théodat, *Long Journey*, 85). In modern Mohawk, *yó:* is an expression of approval of what someone else has just said.

Schene I Atsiehoene may be *skv́:nv vtyóhawe?* 'peace it will bring forth'. *skv́nv* is 'peace', *v-* is the future prefix 'will', *-t-* is the cislocative prefix, in this case meaning 'forth', *yo-* is the pronoun 'it', *-haw-* is the verb root 'to hold', and *-e?* is the aspect suffix.

Netho is *ta?né?tho?* 'so be it!' in modern Mohawk. Compare *etho* 'response of approbation' and *etho* '*oui, bien!*' (Lafitau, *Customs*, 1:298; Cuoq, *Lexique de la langue iroquoise*, 4).

Katon is *kátu?* 'let us consent' in modern Mohawk.

Hỹ is another expression of approval. *Hai* 'hail' also occurs in chants of present-day condolence ceremonies (Tooker, "League of the Iroquois").

84. With this rather blasé statement, especially given the reason for his journey in the first place, Van den Bogaert records that he was a witness to the Oneidas, and presumably to other Iroquois who were present, concluding a peace undoubtedly linked to a trade pact with the French Indians.

85. Onnedaeges is *onutà:ke* 'on the hill', a reference to the Onondagas, Iroquoian-speakers located west of the Oneidas, whose homeland was generally southeast of present-day Syracuse (Blau, Campisi, and Tooker, "Onondaga").

86. Long cloth is duffel.

87. The Indians' grousing about not finding a sufficient supply of trade goods upon reaching Fort Orange was nothing new. A decade earlier, Isaack de Rasières, secretary to the Dutch West India Company, reported: "the Indians will be all the more diligent in hunting [for furs] when they see that when they have skins they can get what they want, about which the Maquaes do not hesitate to complain bitterly, saying: 'Why should we go hunting? Half the time you have no cloth'" (Van Laer, trans. and ed., *Documents Relating*, 231).

88. The translation here is from Dutch to Onondaga through an intermediary. Although related, the Northern Iroquoian languages spoken by the five Iroquois nations are and were, to varying degrees, mutually unintelligible. The most closely related, Mohawk and Oneida, are mutually comprehensible with effort, but Onondaga is sufficiently different as to require translation.

89. Manhatas, a Munsee-language word literally and colloquially translated as 'the place where we get bows', is Manhattan, where the Dutch town of New Amsterdam was built (Goddard, "Manhattan"). The "chief" then at New Amsterdam was Wouter van Twiller, director of New Netherland from 1633 to 1638, the nephew of the patroon Kiliaen van Rensselaer.

90. It is not clear whether the accompanying quotation contains a translation of this word or whether welsmachkoo is only an opening

remark that was not translated. The first two letters, *we-*, constitute a prepronominal prefix, the factual, which in Mohawk generally points to a single event in the immediate past. The letters *-sma-* could be read as *-s(e)wa-*, the pronominal prefix 'you all'. As to the verb base, there is in Mohawk a verb root *-kw-* meaning 'to pick something up from the ground'. This root has an alternate shape *-ko-*, followed by the glottal stop *ʔ* in the punctual aspect. Welsmachkoo could thus be analyzed as *wesewá:koʔ* 'you all picked up'. There is another possibility. The last syllable in welsmachkoo could be the verb *-kv-* 'to see' in the punctual aspect. The result would be *wesewá:kvʔ* 'you all saw it'. Finally, a good case could be made that welsmachkoo is *wesanà:khwvʔ* 'you got angry' in modern Mohawk. Such a rendering appears quite plausible if Van den Bogaert's entry of January 1 is examined. There it says: "An Indian once again called us scoundrels, as has been previously told, and he was very malicious so that Willem Tomassen became so angry that the tears ran from his eyes." The segments of *wesanà:khwvʔ* are the factual prefix *we-*, the objective pronoun *-sa-*, the verb root *-naʔkhwv-* 'to get angry', and the punctual aspect suffix *ʔ*.

91. This Mohawk-language passage contains the first separate listing of the five Iroquois nations in a contemporary record. Also found here may be the earliest known reference to the League of the Iroquois or the Iroquois Confederacy—Kanosoni.

There are two terms for the Iroquois League in the Mohawk language: one is *kanuhsú:ni* 'the built house', and the other is *kanuhsyú:ni* 'the extended house'. The latter form appears to be older and more common than the former (see Goddard's synonymy in Fenton, "Northern Iroquoian Culture Patterns," 320; Bruyas, "Radical Words," 18). It is impossible to know which form Van den Bogaert actually heard at Oneida. It may have been either *kanuhsú:ni* or *kanuhsyú:ni*, which in phonetic rendering is *gunũhsṹ:ni* and *gunũhsṹ:ni* respectively. If he had heard the form *kanushyú:ni*, there is no doubt that the Indians were referring to the Iroquois League. On the other hand, if it was *kanuhsú:ni*, the Indians may have just told him that a house would be built. Nonetheless, given the context and what Van den Bogaert understood regarding what the Indians had told him, it seems certain that the reference was to the League. Following this passage, Van den Bogaert notes that among other things, "I would have a house and fire, wood, and anything else." He does not indicate that anyone would build him a house, but instead, he appears to be saying that he would simply be provided shelter and amenities. However, since the one form is the accepted term for the Iroquois League, while the other could possibly refer to it, there is the strong possibility that this is the earliest record of the League's existence.

Certain oral traditions of Iroquois people today and in the recent past assert that the League was founded much before the arrival of Europeans, perhaps as early as 1,000 years before contact. However, there are documented multiple and independent lines of evidence that point to the League being an early post-contact phenomenon, established sometime in the 1620s (Starna, "League of the Iroquois").

The first two words in the passage refer to white men. The third word, atsimachkoo, may contain the verb root -tsinahk(w)- or possibly -tsina- plus a suffix. Modern Mohawk has a word ratsí:naʔ 'he is a daring fellow'. If this form is followed by the interrogative particle kv, the result is ratsí:naʔkv 'is he a daring fellow?'

It is also possible to analyze atsimachkoo as ratsináhkv 'sorcerer' or 'doctor'. Thus, the possible choices are "is the white man a daring fellow?" or "the white man is a sorcerer." In context, either one of these translations is appropriate. Van den Bogaert, a barber-surgeon, had been asked early in his journey to attend to someone who was ill. The Indians may therefore have referred to him as a white man who was a doctor.

There is little doubt that [-]kaying wee (from OYAKAYING WEE) is kanyv́:ke 'Mohawk'. Megapolensis, writing ten years later, provides "Kajingahaga" 'Mohawk people' (Jameson, ed., Narratives, 172). Also, since Van den Bogaert lists the Iroquois nations from east to west, the word kaying wee correctly precedes the word onneyatte 'Oneidas', who were situated immediately west of the Mohawks.

Finally, it is tempting to equate the last word in this passage, yndicko, with judicha 'conflagration', found in the wordlist. However, this would be somewhat tenuous. Consequently, a blank is left.

A possible rendering of the passage is as follows:

HA ASSIRONI	ATSIMACHKOO	KENT	O/YA/KAYING WEE
ra?serúni	*ratsí:na?kʋ*	*kʋ*:tho*	*ká:yʋ kanyʋ*:ke*
The white man	is he a daring fellow?	here	it is Mohawk
	ratsináhkʋ		
	is a sorcerer/doctor		

ONNEYATTE	ONAONDAGE	KOYOCKWE	HOO SENOTO	WANY/AGWEGAN/NE HOO
onʋ*:yote?	*onutà:ke*	*koyó:kwʋ*	*hotinutó:wane?*	*thiwakwé:ku*
Oneida	Onondaga	Cayuga	Seneca	all over

SCHENE/HALTON	KASTEN	KANOSONI	YNDICKO
skʋ*:nʋ horá:tu	*kástha?*	*kanuhsyú:ni*	
safely he is lying down	it is useful	Iroquois League	

The gloss of this passage is obviously disjointed and undoubtedly represents only a fragment of what had been a much longer statement by the Indians, one that Van den Bogaert struggled to record. The significance of this passage has not been previously recognized. Certainly, General Wilson, the original translator, was not aware of its meaning in Mohawk, choosing only to translate Van den Bogaert's Dutch. Soon after the journal's initial publication, Beauchamp ("Indian Nations," 322) noted that the passage contained the names of the Iroquois' "castles," Onneyatte, Onaondage, Koyockure, and "the two Seneca castles of Honotowany and Senenehalaton, apparently forms of Souontouane and Tiotobaton." However, Beauchamp's translation was partially inaccurate. Moreover, he was unaware of a transcription error committed by Wilson. In the original, Wilson ("Corlaer and His Journal" and "Arent Van Curler") transcribed the word "Kanosoni" as "Franosoni," which, in addition to his slip of the pen, is not a Mohawk sound sequence (see also Jameson, ed., *Narratives*, 152). For more on the League, consult Tooker, "League of the Iroquois," and especially Fenton, *Great Law*.

92. Today, as in the past, rattles, most often made from the shells of snapping turtles (*Chelydra serpentina*), are used to accompany singers and dancers in Iroquois ritual and ceremony. Contemporary craftsmen use chokecherry pits, corn kernels, or small pebbles to produce

the rattling sound, perhaps the same materials used for Van den Bogaert's "beads" (Fenton, *False Faces*, 191–96).

93. Bunches of corn were hung to dry from the rafters of long-houses as part of food storage technology.

94. Sucking, and also blowing, as curative practices, were found among Iroquoians and other North American Indians (see Tooker, *Huron Indians*, 117). The otter (skin) may have been the personal charm of the sick person or one of the healers.

95. The stone that Van den Bogaert said was scarce, which rules out the ubiquitous and plentiful chert (commonly called flint) found on period archaeological sites, was probably pyrite, or iron pyrite. During the sixteenth and seventeenth centuries, pyrite was used as an ignition source for European-manufactured wheel locks, a weapon that was eventually replaced by the flintlock musket. Indians started their fires with sparks thrown by striking pyrite against a piece of chert, called a strike-a-light by archaeologists.

96. Sinck, a Sinneken (see note 1).

97. Onondagas.

98. This man's name contains the Onondaga noun root -*nast*- 'rafter', with the remainder indecipherable (Hanni Woodbury, personal communication, 2011).

99. This is Onondaga Lake, which the French could have reached by boating up the Oswego River.

100. This may be a reference to either the Delaware or the Susquehanna River and the European settlements there.

101. Satteeu is sateen, an English name for a cotton fabric commonly used in making linings.

102. Snowshoe hare (*Lepus americanus*).

103. See note 50.

104. See note 48.

105. See note 44.

106. See note 44.

107. This is Arenias. See note 80.

108. See note 42.

109. Taturot, in modern Mohawk, would be *thothú:rote?* 'he has a gun standing at his side'. It contains the noun root *-hur-* 'blowgun' and the verb root *-ot-* 'to be standing'.

110. The Mahicans, an Algonquian-speaking people resident in the Hudson and upper Housatonic Valleys, referred to by the Dutch as Mahikanders (see Starna, *Homeland to New Land*; Bradley, *Before Albany*). On the Mohawk-Mahican War, during which this village was abandoned, see Starna and Brandão, "Mohawk-Mahican War."

WORDLIST

 $\mathcal{T}$ he following wordlist, found at the end of Van den Bogaert's journal, is the earliest known philological treatment of the Mohawk language in existence. Its author deserves high praise for recording a vocabulary of such quality, especially considering the conditions under which the list was made and the fact that he was interacting with people who spoke a language that was utterly exotic when compared to his own.

The wordlist is arranged as follows: The left-hand column provides Van den Bogaert's rendering of the Mohawk language as he heard and recorded it, while the column on the right contains the transcription of the Dutch equivalent, followed by an English gloss. These data were provided by Charles T. Gehring and William A. Starna, editors of this volume. On the next line, and in brackets, I have furnished the modern Mohawk equivalent with an English gloss, where possible.

As the reader will note, there are a number of words which could not be identified by native speakers of Mohawk. Also, it is obvious that Van den Bogaert's queries about language did not always elicit the desired response. For example, at some point he asked a question aimed at learning the word or phrase for "immediately." The answer was "not yet." It is not surprising that the manner of asking a question about an object or concept would, at times, cause confusion, both on the Dutchman's part

and that of the Indians. Where appropriate, I have made observations regarding some of these difficulties.

The letter "v" represents a nasal vowel comparable to the *on*
in French *maison*; the symbol "?" represents a glottal stop; ":" is
vowel length; "'" is a rising tone; and "`" is a falling tone.
I wish to express my gratitude to Mike Norton, Catherine
Norton, and Frank Natawe, of Kahnawake, Quebec, for their
expert help in identifying Mohawk words and phrases.

GUNTHER MICHELSON

Maquase spraeck [Mohawk language]	Nederlanse spraeck [Dutch language]	
assire oft oggaha [*áhsire?* 'blanket'] [*okúha?*] 'felt' (material)	duffels laecken	'cloth'
atoga [*ató:kv?* 'axe']	Byllen	'axes'
atsochta [*atsò:ktv?* 'hoe']	dissels	'adzes'
assere [*à:share?* 'knife']	messen	'knives'
assaghe [*áhsikwe?* 'spear']	rappie(r) lennet	'rapier'
attochwat [*atókwa?* 'spoon']	leepels	'spoons'
ondach [*ú:tak* 'kettle']	ceetels	'kettles'
endathatst [*yutatkóhstha?* 'mirror']	spyegels	'looking glass'
tasaskarisat [*tewata?sharì:sas* 'scissors']	schaeren	'scissors'
kamrewari [*kanú:ware?* 'awls'] [*karú:ware?* 'awls']	Elsen ysers	'awls'
onekoera [*o?nekórha?* 'wampum']	sewant haer geldt	'sewan, their money'

tiggeretait   cammen   'combs'
    [*atkerothí:ha*ʔ 'comb']
catse   Bellen   'bell'
    [*kátshe*ʔ 'jar']
Dedaia Witha   hemden ofte   'shirts or
    [*atyà:tawi* 'shirt', 'jacket']   rocken   coats'
nonnewarory   karpoesen mussen   'fur cap'
    [*anù:warore*ʔ 'hat']
Eytroghe   craelen   'beads'
    [*ohstarò:kwa*ʔ 'large beads']
Canagoesat   Schraepers   'scraper'
    [*ohnakóhsa*ʔ 'deer hide']¹
Caris   Cousen   'stocking'
    [*ká:ris* 'stockings']
achta   schoenen   'shoes'
    [*áhta*ʔ 'shoe']

Naemen van beesten soo daer vallen
[Names of animals found there]

aque   harten   'deer'²
aquesados   paerden   'horses'
    [*akohsá:tʋs* 'horse']
adiron   katten   'cats'
    [*atì:ru* 'raccoon']³
aquidagon   Juck hoorn   'oxen'⁴
senotowanne   Elant   'elk'
    [*oskenutó:wane*ʔ 'elk']
ochquari   Beeren   'bear'
    [*ohkwá:ri*ʔ 'bear']
sinite   bever   'beaver'
    [*tsyaní:to* 'beaver']
tawyne   otter   'otter'
    [*tawí:ne* 'otter']
eyo   Minck   'mink'
    [*ayó:ha*ʔ 'mink']
senadondo   vos   'fox'⁵
ochquoha   wolf   'wolf'
    [*okwáho*ʔ 'wolf']
seranda   Mater   'marten'⁶

Ichar *or* sateeni	hondt	'dog'
[*è:rhar* 'dog']		
[*satshé:nv?* 'your domestic		
animal']		
tali	kraen	'crane'[7]
kragequa	swaen	'swan'
kahanckt	gans	'geese'
[*káhuk* 'wild goose']		
schawariwane	kallekoen	'turkey'
[*skaweró:wane?* 'turkey']		
schascariwanasi	Arent	'eagle'
tantanege	haes	'hare'
[*tauhtané:kv* 'rabbit']		
onckwe	mensen	'men'
[*ú:kwe* 'human being']		
etsi	een man	'a man'
[*rà:tsin* 'a male animal']		
coenheckti	een vrou	'a woman'
[*o?nhétyv* 'a female		
animal']		
ochtaha	een oudt man	'an old man'
[*rokstvha* 'an old man']		
odasqueta	een oude vrou	'an old woman'[8]
sine gechtera	een vryer	'a young man'
[*senekvhteru* 'you are a		
young man']		
exhechta	een vryster	'a young girl'
[*eksà:?a* 'a girl']		
ragina	een vader	'father'
[*ráke?ni* 'father']		
distan	een moeder	'mother'
[*istv:?a* 'mother']		
Cian	een Kint	'child'
[*riyv:?a* 'my son']		
rocksongwa	een jongen	'boy'
[*raksà:?a* 'a boy']		
cannawarori	een hoer	'prostitute'
[*yonuhwaró:ri* 'she has		
loose morals']		

Oentar [*onuhtè:ra?* 'a support']⁹	een swaere vrou	'woman in labor', 'pregnant woman'
ragenonou [*rakenohà:?a* 'my uncle']	Oom	'uncle'
rackesie [*raktsì:?a* 'my older brother']¹⁰	Cousyn	'cousin'
anochquis [*onúhkwis* 'hair']	het haeyr	'hair'
anonsi [*onú:tsi* 'head']	het hooft	'head'
ochochta [*ohúhta?* 'ear']	de oren	'ears'
ohonckwa [*ohù:kwa?* 'throat'] [*onyà:kwa?* 'throat']	de keel	'throat'
oneyatsa [*o?nyúhsa?* 'nose']	de nues	'nose'
owanisse [*awv?náhsu* 'its tongue']	de tongh	'tongue'
onawy [*onawí:ra?* 'tooth']	de tanden	'teeth'
onenta [*onútsha?* 'arm']	de nermen	'arms'
osnotsa [*osnúhsa?* 'hand']	de handen	'hands'
onatassa	de vingeren	'fingers'
otichkera	den duyem	'thumb'
otsira [*otsi?é:ra?* 'fingernail']	de naegelen	'nails'
onirare [*onerà:rha?* 'shoulder blade']	het schouder blaedt	'shoulder blade'
orochquine [*oruhkwé:na?* 'spine']	het rugge been	'spine'
ossidau [*ohsì:ta?* 'foot']	de voeten	'feet'

onera	vroulyckheyt	'vagina'
[yené:ru 'she is pregnant']		
oeuda	Menschen dreck	'excrement'
[óʔtaʔ 'excrement']		
onsaha	de blaes	'bladder'
canderes	mandelyckheyt	'phallus'[11]
awasta	de klooten	'testicles'
casoya	een schip schuyt &	'ship' and
	kanoo	'canoe'
canossade	een huys ofte	'house' or
[kanúhsoteʔ 'there is a	hutte	'hut'
house']		
onega	waeter	'water'
[ohné:kaʔ 'a liquid']		
oetseira	vier	'fire'
[ó:tsireʔ 'fire']		
oyente	hout brant hout	'wood',
[ó:yvteʔ 'wood']		'firewood'
osconte	bast van boomen	'bark'
[oskú:taraʔ 'sheet of bark']		
canadera	broodt	'bread'
[kanà:taro 'bread']		
ceheda	boonen	'beans'
[osahè:taʔ 'beans']		
oneste	Mayeys	'maize'
[ó:nvhsteʔ 'corn']		
cinsie	vis	'fish'
[kútsyuʔ 'fish']		
Ghekeront	sallem	'salmon'
[kaké:ru 'they lie on the		
ground'][12]		
oware	vlees	'meat'
[oʔwà:ruʔ 'meat']		
athesera	meel	'flour'
[othè:seraʔ 'flour']		
satsori	eeten	'to eat'
[satshó:ri 'slurp']		
onighira	drincken	'to drink'
[vkhnekí:raʔ 'I shall drink']		

Kattenkerreyager
[*vkatuhkárya ʔke ʔ* 'I shall be
hungry']

augustuske
[*vkewístoske ʔ* 'I get cold']

oyendere
[*yoyánere* 'it is good']

rockste

jachteyendere
[*yáhte yoyánere* 'it is not
good']

quane
[*kowá:nv* 'large']

canyewa
[*kv ʔniwà: ʔa* 'it is small']

wotstaha

cates
[*kà:tvs* 'it is thick']

satewa
[*sha ʔté:wa* 'it is of the
same size']¹³

sagat
[*neshá:kat* 'the same' (two
things)]

Awaheya
[*yawvhé:yu* 'she is dead']

aghihi
[*akíheye ʔ* 'I could die']

sastorum
[*satsnó:rat* 'hurry up!']

archoo
[*á:rekho* 'not yet']

owaetsei
[*uwà:stsi* 'á little while
ago']

thederri
[*thetó:re* 'yesterday']

Jorhani
[*vyórhv ʔne ʔ* 'tomorrow']

grooten honger — 'very hungry'

heel kout — 'very cold'

heel goedt — 'very good'

vriendt vrienden — 'friends'
ten duecht niet — 'tis no good'

Groot — 'large'

kleyn — 'small'

Breet — 'broad'
dick — 'thick'

alleens — 'alone'

dubbelt — 'doubly'

doot — 'death'

sieck — 'sick'

haest u wat — 'hurry up'

daetelyck — 'immediately'

neu — 'now'

Gisteren — 'yesterday'

morgen — 'tomorrow'

62   WORDLIST

careyago	de lucht	'the light'
[*karuhyà:ke* 'in the sky']		
karackwero	de sonne	'the sun'
[*karáhkwa* 'sun']		
Asistock	de sterren	'the stars'
[*otsíhsto* 'star']		
sintho	saeyen	'(to) plant'
[*tsyútho* 'sow']		
deserentekar	weyden	'(to) graze'
sorsar	Aen hoogen	'to raise'
Cana	saet	'seed'
[*kà:nv* 'seed']		
onea	steen	'stone'
[*onú:ya* 'stone']		
Canadack *or* Cany	een sack oft mant	'sack or
[*kahnà:ta* 'purse']		basket'
Canadaghi	een Casteel	'a castle'
[*kanatà:ke* 'in the village']		
oÿoghi	een Kill	'a waterway'
[*kayúha* 'creek']		
canaderage	een revier	'a river'
[*kanyatarà:ke* 'on the lake']		
Johati	een padt oft wegh	'a path or
[*tyohá:te* 'there is a path']		road'
onstara	huylen	'cry'
[*yutstárha* 'they weep']		
aquayesse	lachen	'laugh'
[*yukwayéshu* 'we are chuckling']		
ohonte	Groente gras	'greens',
[*óhute* 'grass']		'grass'
oneggeri	riet oft stroey	'reed' or
[*onékeri* 'hay']		'straw'
Christittye	yser cooper loot	'iron',
[*karístatsi* 'iron']		'copper',
		'lead'
onegonsera	roode verve	'red paint'
[*onekwúhtara* 'red'][14]		
cahonsye	swart	'black'
[*kahù:tsi* 'black']		

Crage	witt	'white'
[karà:kʋ 'white']		
ossivenda	blau	'blue'
[otyarò:ta 'orange-colored']		
endatcondere	schildren	'(to) paint'
[okúhtshera ? 'the paint']		
Joddireyo	vechten	'(to) fight'
[yuterí:yos 'they fight']		
Aquinachoo	Quaet	'angry'
[aukenà:khwʋ ? 'I would get angry']		
Jaghacteroene	vervaert	'afraid'
[yakohterù:ni 'she is afraid']		
dadeneye	speelen dubbelen	'to gamble'
[tvtení:yʋ 'I bet you']		
asserie	heel sterck	'very strong'
[ahserí:ye ? 'a rope']¹⁵		
carente	slim of krom	'sly or bad'
[wakahrò:re ? 'it is crooked']		
odossera	speck	'bacon'
[o ?túsera ? 'the fat']		
keye	vet	'fat'
[kò:ye 'lard']		
wistotcera	smeer	'grease'
[owistóhsera ? 'butter']		
ostie	been	'bone'
[óhstyʋ 'bone']		
aghidawe	slaepen	'sleep'
[aukí:ta ?we ? 'I would sleep']		
sinekaty	by slaepen	'(to have) intercourse'
[se ?neká:ta ? 'your crotch area']		
Jankanque	heel moey	'very beautiful'
[yakú:kwe 'a woman']		
atsochwat	Toback	'tobacco'
[katshókwas 'I smoke']		

canonou [*kanv̀:nawv̀ʔ* 'tobacco pipe']	Tobacks pyp	'tobacco pipe'
esteronde [*waʔostarú:ti ̀ʔ* 'it started to rain']	reegen	'(to) rain'
waghideria [*wakaʔtarihv́:ʔv* 'I am perspiring']	sweeten	'(to) sweat'
kayontochke [*kahvtà:ke* 'on the meadow']	vlac saeylant	'flat, arable land'
ononda [*onú:ta ̀ʔ* 'mountain']	Bergen	'mountain'
Cayanoghe [*kawehnò:ke* 'on the island']	eylanden	'islands'
schahohadee [*skaháhati* 'the other side of the road']	de over syede	'the reverse side'
caroo [*kà:ro* 'closer to me']	hier nae toe	'nearby'
cadadiiene [*katatyv́:ni* 'I am storing it for myself']	handelen	'(to) trade'
daweyate [*takatáweyaʔteʔ* 'I entered']	raet houden	'(to) hold council'
agotsioha	een kraeles arm	'a string of beads'
aquayanderen [*yukwayá:ner* 'we are chiefs']	een oversten	'a chief'
seronquatse [*shrukwehtáksv ̀ʔ* 'a really evil person']	een schellem	'a scoundrel'
sariwacksi [*serihwáksv ̀ʔ* 'your ways are bad']	een kakelaer	'a blasphemer'

onewachten
[*ronowóhtu* 'he has told
lies']

tenon commeyon
[*tonvkú:yu?* 'how much
shall I give you?']

sinachkoo
[*hatsináhkv* 'exorcist']¹⁶

adenocquat
[*vhatenúhkwa?te?* 'he will
give medicine']

coenhaseren
[*kuhnhà:sere?* 'I am here to
heal you']¹⁷

sategat
[*saté:ka?t* 'light the fire!']

judicha
[*yotékha?* 'it is burning']

catteges issewe
[*kátke tutésewe?* 'when will
you all come back']

tesenochte
[*tvhsanúhtu?* 'do as you
like']

tegenhonid
[*tvyokvhnhú:ti* 'the season
when everything opens
up']

otteyage

augustuske
[*vkewístoske?* 'I shall get
cold']

katkaste
[*katkátstus* 'I make soup']

jori
[*yó:ri* 'it is cooked']

dequoquoha
[*tewakóha* 'let's go and get
it!']

een logenaer 'a liar'

wat wilt ghy 'what do you
hebben want'

duyvel jaegen '(to) exorcise
the devil'

medecyn salven '(to) make
medicine'

gesont maecken '(to) heal'

lecht hout aen vier '(to) ignite
wood'

het brandt 'conflagration'

wanneer comt ghy 'when shall
weer you return'

ick weet het niet 'I do not
know'

int voor jaer 'in the
spring'

den soomer 'the summer'
den winter 'the winter'

eeten kooken '(to) cook
food'

het is gaer 'it is cooked'

wt jaegen gaen 'to go out
hunting'

osqucha	ick salt haelen	'I shall fetch it'
[*vhskóha*? 'you will get it']		
seyendereii	ick kan hen wel	'I know them well'
[*seyvterì:*?*u* 'you recognize the person']		
kristoni asseroni	Nederlanders	'Dutch'
[*keristú:ni* 'I am a metal-maker']	duytsen	
[*o*?*serú:ni* 'axe-maker, European, French']¹⁸		
aderondackx	fransen of	'French or
[*atirú:taks* 'Algonquin Indians', 'Ojibway Indians']¹⁹	engelsen	English'
anesagghena	Mahikanders	'Mahikanders'
[*ronatshá:kanv* 'Eastern Algonquians']²⁰		
torsas	omde nooert	'to the north'
[*othorè:ke* 'north']		
Kanonnewage	de manhatas	'the
[*kanú:no wà:ke*? 'I go to New York City (Manhattan)']		Manhatas (Manhattan)'
onscat	1 Een	'one'
[*úska*]		
tiggeni	2 Twee	'two'
[*tékeni*]		
asse	3 dree	'three'
[*áhsv*]		
cayere	4 vier	'four'
[*kayé:ri*]		
wisck	5 vyef	'five'
[*wisk*]		
jayack	6 ses	'six'
[*yà:ya*?*k*]		
tsadack	7 seeven	'seven'
[*tsyá:ta*]		
hategon	8 Acht	'eight'
[*sha*?*té:ku*]		

tyochte [*tyóhtu*]	9	neegen	'nine'
oyere [*oyé:ri*]	10	Tien	'ten'
tawasse [*tewáhsv* '20']	40	veertich	'forty'
onscatteneyawe [*vskatewvˀnyáweˀ*]	100	hondert	'one-hundred'

NOTES

1. Van den Bogaert asked, or possibly gestured, to learn the word for a tool being used to scrape a deer hide. Through an obvious misunderstanding, he was provided the word for the hide being scraped.

2. The modern Mohawk word for deer is *oskenú:tu*. However, there is good reason to believe that Van den Bogaert actually heard the word *aque*, which must have been in use among the Mohawks at the time. Cognates of *aque* are found in Tuscarora, *á:kweh*, in the now extinct Susquehannock language, *haagw*, and in Cherokee, *ahwi*. All of these terms are traceable to proto-Iroquoian (Mithun, "Proto-Iroquoians," 265).

3. Van den Bogaert was unsure what to call an animal that did not occur in Europe. However, since a raccoon apparently looked to him like an exotic cat, he settled on the word "cat."

4. In modern Mohawk there is an animal term that matches exactly Van den Bogaert's entry for oxen. This is *ukwetá:ku*, but it means 'squirrel'.

5. This is another case where Van den Bogaert recorded a term that has since disappeared from the Mohawk language. In modern Mohawk "fox" is *tsítshoˀ*. Old Huron had the term *Tsinantononq*, a fox, cognate of Van den Bogaert's *senadondo* (Sagard-Théodat, *Long Journey*, 222).

6. The modern Mohawk term for "marten" is *onú:kote?*. It is conceivable that Van den Bogaert had heard and recorded the word *seranda* from a member of the Onondaga delegation while he was at the Oneida village. In a seventeenth-century French-Onondaga dictionary, marten (*marte/martre*) is listed as *tcherannoha*, which could be a cognate of Van den Bogaert's *seranda* (Shea, ed., *French-Onondaga Dictionary*, 69).

7. Van den Bogaert heard a term that is no longer used by Mohawk speakers. In modern Mohawk, "crane" is *tehkáhu*. Old Huron *taron* 'duck' is a cognate of *tali* 'cranes' (Sagard-Théodat, *Long Journey*, 221).

8. The modern Mohawk word for "old woman" is *akokstúha*. Laurentian, another northern Iroquoian language that was recorded by the French explorer Jacques Cartier in 1535–1536, and is now extinct, had the term *Aggouette* 'women', which could be cognate to Van den Bogaert's *odasqueta* (Biggar, ed., *Voyages of Jacques Cartier*, 242).

9. Perhaps the Mohawks wanted to express the idea that a woman in labor requires "support" or "a support."

10. In the Iroquois kinship system, a male parallel first cousin would be recognized by other parallel first cousins as a sibling, either an older or younger brother, or in the case of females, a younger or older sister.

11. *Canderes* could not be identified by Mohawk informants, however, old Onondaga has "*Gánneris*," that is, "man's genitals" (Zeisberger, *Zeisberger's Indian Dictionary*, 82).

12. Rather than learning the name of the fish he was pointing to or gesturing at, Van den Bogaert was provided their disposition.

13. This is an excellent example of the difficulties one can encounter in attempting to elicit responses regarding language concepts.

14. Compare *Ogsentsera* '*peinture rouge*' (Bruyas, "Radical Words," 52).

15. The inquiry here was directed at learning what the word for rope was. Instead, the Indian questioned referred to the rope's strength, its quality.

16. See journal note 59.

17. Another equivalent in modern Mohawk may be *kuyunhahse-rú:ni* 'I make you healthy again'.

18. *Asseroni* "axe-makers" is a reference to any European. On Canadian reserves today it applies in particular to the French. The Mohawk name for the English became *tyorhvʔshá:kaʔ*, which means 'daylighters' or 'easterners', or simply, 'orientals'.

19. Van den Bogaert's *Aderondackx*, or Adirondacks, were the Algonquins of the Ottawa Valley and environs (Day and Trigger, "Algonquin," 797). Lafitau, *Customs*, 2:62, wrote that "the Iroquois give the Algonquin the name of *Rontaks*, that is to say, *Tree Eaters*."

20. The *Anesaggena*, that is, the Mahicanders, or Mahicans, were mentioned again in the 1640s by the Dutch clergyman Johannes Megapolensis, who referred to them as "Mahakans, otherwise called *Agotzagena*" (Jameson, ed., *Narratives*, 172). Thirty years later, "Mahingan" is listed by Bruyas, who also knew these Indians under the name "*ratsagannha.*" He translated "*Atsagannen*" as "*parler une langue étrangère*" (Bruyas, "Radical Words," 28, 42). *Ratsagannha* and comparable forms were later applied to other Algonquian-speaking groups living east and southeast of the Mohawks. "Mahican," "Mahikander," "Maikens," and others are names that seem to have resulted from the early Dutch use of Munsee-speaking interpreters who pronounced the name *mà·hí·kan, mà·hí·kani·w,* Mahíkanak. See synonymy in Brasser, "Mahican," 211.

LOOFT GODT BOVEN AL OPT FORT ORAENGIEN 1634

11 December[:] Memoriael gehouden vande voornaem-
ste dingen die myn voorgevallen syn int reysen nae de
maquasen & sinnekens vooreerst soo waeren de reeden
waer om dat wy gongen dese als dat de maquasen & sinnekens by onse Commys Marten Gerritsen & myn dickwils hadden comen seggen dat daer franse wilden In haer
landt waeren & datse treves met haer gemaek[t] hadden
so dat sy daer te weeten de maquasen met haer vellen
wilden handelen omdat de maquasen soo veel voor haer
vellen wouden hebben als de france wilden wouden hebben soo heb Ick aenden Sr. Marten Gerritsen versocht om
datwaers te gaen & de waerheyt daer van te vernemen
om den E.H.M. soo drae tegen te loopen als mede & dat
het heel dubegue[s] met den handel stont soo ben ick dat
nu als boven met Jeromus la Croex & Willem Tomassen
gegaen de heere wilde reyse segenen tusschen :9:a:10:
vren gongen met :5: maquasen wilden meest noort west
aen & nae 8 mylen gaens quaemen wy 1/2 vre inden avont
in een Jaegers huysken daer wy dien nacht slypen by den
offal die in haer landt loopt & wert genaemt OYOGE de
wilden gaven ons hier te eeten haerten vlees het landt is

hier meest vol greenen boomen & veel vlack landt desen
offal loopt by haer Casteel in haers landt maer cunnen
die niet op vaeren door de groote afwateringhe[.]

12 ditto[:] :3: vren voorden dage soo gongen wy weder
onser reyse te vorderen & die wilden die met ons gegaen
waeren souden ons daer hebben laeten blyven soo Ick het
niet gewaer hadde geworden & doen wy wat meenden
te eeten doen hadden haere honden ons vlees en onse
caes opgegeten soo dat wy doen maer droogh Broot hadden & mosten daer op gaen & nae dat wy een vre gegaen
hadden soo quamen wy inde spruyt die in onse revier
loopt & verby de maquasen haer steeden hier gongh al
harden ys gangh Jeronimus die voor hier eerst over met
een wilt in een canoo van bast van bomen met een wilt
want daer conden maer 2 man seffens in vaeren daer nae
Willem & ick & het was soo doncker dat wy malcander
niet sien en conden of mosten dichtby malcander coomen
soodat soodat [sic] het niet sonder preyckel en was & doen
wy over gevaren waeren soo gongen wy noch 1 1/2 myle
& quamen in een Jaegers huysken daer wy ingongen &
aten daer wat harten vlees & spoeden weder onse reyse
& nadat wy noch een 1/2 myl gegaen hadden soo saegen
wy enich volck nae ons toe coemen & doen sy ons saegen doen lypen sy wech & smeeten haer sacken & packen
wech liepen in een valey & achter een creupel bos dat
wy haer niet en saegen wy besaegen haer goet & packen
namen daer een brootken van & was met boonen gebacken dat wy op aten & gongen doen almeest langs dese
voornoemde kill die seer vreselyck lyep van afwateringh
hier in dese kil leggen veel eylanden & aen weer syden wel

:500:a:600: morgen vlacklant jae noch wel meer & doen
wy soo by gissinge 11 mylen gegaen hadden quamen een
vre in den avont 1/2 myl van eerste Casteel in een huysken daer anders niemant in was dan vrouwen wy souden
doen wel voort aen gegaen hebben maer ick conde myn
voeten niet versetten door het moeyelyck gaen so dat wy
daer doen slypen was seer coudt met noorde windt[.]

13 ditto[:] gongen wy smorgens met malcanderen nae
het Casteel overt Eys dat dese nacht inde kil gevrosen was
& doen wy 1/2 myl gegaen hadden quaemen wy in haer
eerste Casteel dat op eenen hoogen bergh leyt daer stonden maer :36: huysen reygh aen reygh straets gewyse dat
wy daer moey door conden gaen dese huysen syn gemaeckt & gedeckt met basten van boomen loopen boven meest
pladt de sommige syn :100:90:80: treeden langh :22:a:23
voeten hooge daer waeren mede enige binnen dueren
van gekloof de plancken daer ysere henghsels aen waeren
wy saegen in sommege huysen mede yserwerck ysere ket-
tingen bouts egghe tanden eysere hoepen spyckers dat
sy steelen als sy hier van daen gaen hier was het meeste
volck wt jaegen om Beeren & harten dese huysen waeren
vol cooren dat sy ONESTI heeten & wy mayeys jae inde
sommige wel :300:a:400 scheepel sy maecken scheepen
ende tonnen van bast van boomen & mayent met bast
van boomen wy aten hier veel pompoenen gebraden &
gesooden die sy ANONSIRA noemen daer waeren geen
oversten thuys maer den oppersten sey ADRIOCHTEN
genaemt die woonden 1/4 myl van fort in een kleyn huysken wt oorsaecke dat hier int Casteel veel wilden vande
Cinder pocken gestoruen waeren ick liet hem ontbieden

dat hy by my soude comen het welcke hy dede quam ende hieten my wellekoem & nooden ons dat hy gaeren woude dat wy mette hem souden gaen wy souden gegaen hebben maer wy werden van een andere Overste geroepen doen wy al op den wegh waeren & keerden wederom naet Casteel die liet stracks een groot vier aen leggen & eenen vetten harten bout koocken daer wy van aeten & gaf ons mede :2: beeren huyden om op te slaepen & schonck myn 3 Pr. beuers & op den avont doen werden in Willem Tomassen syn been enige sneeden gesneden met een mes alsoo vant gaen geswollen was & daer nae soo werden t gesmeert met beeren smeer wy sliepen hier in dit huys aeten hier veel pompoenen boonen & harten vlees so dat wy hier geen honger leeden maer hadden t soo goet alst hier in haer landt valt hoope dat alles wel sal gelucken[.]

Den 14 ditto[:] schreef Jeronimus een brief aen den Commys Marten Gerritsen ontboodt daer mede pampier soudt & ATSOCHWAT dat is wilden toback wy gongen om te sien of wy geen Callekoenen conden schieten met den Oversten maer conde geen becomen doch op den avont coft ick een seer vette Callekoen voor 2 handt sew[ant] die den oversten voor ons koockten & het smeer dat daer van Coockten dat dede hy ons in boonen & in mayeys desen Oversten liet myn syen afgodt sien het welck een maters hooft was daer de tanden uyt steecken & was bekleet met root duffels laecken den eenen houdt een slangh een schilpadt swaen kraen duyf & diergelycke dingen voor syn afgodt af waer seggen duncken dat sy dan altyt geluck sullen hebben hier gongen :2: wilden met vellen naet fort Oraengien[.]

Den 15 ditto[:] doen gong ick met den Oversten weder uyt callecoenen jaegen maer kreegen geen & op den avont doen liet ons den Oversten weder syn afgodt sien & namen voor ons noch 2 a 3 dagen hier te blyven tot dat de gelegentheyt presenteerde om verder te gaen door den grooten sneu & sonder padt[.]

Den 16 ditto[:] naeden middach quam hier by ons een goeden jaeger SICKARIS genaemt die ons met gewelt mede wilden hebben & ons goet draegen nae syn Caste[el] presenteerde ons dat wy in syn huys souden slaepen & daer soo lange blyven als ons soude gelieven & om dat hy ons soo veel presenteerde soo schonck ick hem een mes met twe elsen ysers & den Oversten daer wy te vooren thuys gelegen hadden schonck ick een mes met een schaer & soo naemen wy ons afgescheyt van dit Casteel ONEKA-HONCKA & naedat wy 1/2 myl gegaen hadden over teys soo saegen wy een dorp daer maer :6: huysen stonden & was genaemt CANOWARODE maer wy gongen daer niet in alsoo hy seyde dat die niet veel dochten & naedat wy noch 1/2 myl gegaen hadden soo gongen wy weder verby een dorp daer :12: huysen in stonden & was genaemt SCHATSYEROSY dese waeren mede gelyck de anderen seggende mede dat die niet veel dochten & naedat wy weder :1: myl oft anderhalf gegaen hadden verby groote stucken vlacklandt so quaemen wy in dit Castell met dat het wel :2: vren inden avondt was ick en conde anders niet sien dan veel doot graeuen dit Casteel is genaemt CAN-AGERE het leyt mede op een bergh sonder pallesaden ofte enigh beschut hier waeren maer 7 mannen thuys & een party oude vrouwen en kinderen den Oversten van

dit Casteel TONNOSATTON & TANIWEROT waeren wt
jagen soodat wy inden SECKARISEN huys sliepen gelyck
hy ons belooft hadde & telden in syn huys :120 pr. lever-
baer bevers die hy met sy eygen honden gevangen hadden
wy aeten hier alle daegen me bevers vleys in dit Casteel
staen :16: huysen langh .50.60.70.80. treden langh & een
van 16 treden & een van vyf treden daer een beer in stondt
om te mesten & hadde daer wel :3: jaeren ingestanden &
was soo mack dat hy al dat wat men hem gaff te eete[.]

Den 17 ditto[:] Sonnedach besaegen wy ons goedt &
quaemen by een pampier met swavel & Jeronimus die die
[*sic*] nam daer wat van & smeet het op het vier sy sagen
den blauwen vlam ende roocken den rueck ende seyden
ons dat sy mede sulck goedt hadden & doen SICKARIS
inquam verhaelden syt ons dat wy haer dat eens souden
laeten sien & het was alleen wy vraeghden hem hoe hy
daer aen quam seyde ons dat syt van de vreemde wilden
hadden & dat syt voor veele siekten goedt hielden maer
principael voor haer beenen als die heel seer doen vant
gaen & seer moede syn[.]

Den 18 ditto[:] Quaemen hier 3 vrouwen van de sinnekens met salm die drooge waeren & oonoch nat waeren
maer die stoncken seer & vercoften ider salm voor een
gulden of :2: handt seewant sy brochten mede vele groene
toback om daer te vercoopen & hadden :6: daegen onder
weegen geweest & conden alhaer salm hier niet vercoopen maer gongen daer mede naet eerste Casteel &
dan souden wy met haer gaen als sy weder quaemen &
op den avont soo seyde my Jeronimus dat hem een wilt
meenden doot te steecken met een mes[.]

Den 19 ditto[:] Kreegen wy een brieff van Marten
Gerritsen gedat[eert] van den achtienden deses kreegen
daer mede pampier sout ende toback voor den wilden
& een flesken met brande wyn & heverden een man dat
onse gidse wesen sou naede sinnekens & gaven hem 1/2
@ duffel :2: pr. bylen :2: messen & :2: pr. elsens eysers
hadt het soomer geweest daer soude volck genoech mede
gegaen hebben maer door dien dat winter was wouden
niet wt haer landt gaen om dat het daer dickwils een
mans lenckte sneeut wy hadden desen dach seer grooten
reegen & ick gaf desen wilt een paer schoenen & hieten
hy SQORHEA[.]

Adi 20 ditto[:] Doen gongen wy vandt :2:de Casteel &
doen wy :1: myl gegaen hadden doen quaem onsen wilt
SQORHEA voor een offal daer wy mosten gaen desen
offal daer liep seer hardt afwater & met veel grooten
schoeten eys wandt door den grooten regen van gisteren
soo was den offal opgebroocken soo dat wy daer in groot
preykel waeren wandt hadde daer maer een van ons gevallen die hadde om den hals geweest doch Godt de heer
bewaerden ons & quaemen daer duer waeren nat tot den
middel toe & doen wy weder een half myl gegaen hadden
quaemen wy soo nat bevroren met onse cleeren cousen
schoenen op een seer hooghen bergh daer :32: huysen
stonden alle gelyck de voorgaende waeren de sommege
langh :100:90:80: treeden of stappen in yder huys waeren
:4:5:a:6 steeden daer gevuyr & gekoockt warden hier
waeren veel wilden tuys soo dat wy hier veel besiens hadden van ouden van de jongen jae wy conden hyer haest
niet door de wilden gaen sy drongen malcander int vier

om ons te sien & het wel midder nacht was altoos eer sy
van ons scheyden wy conden ons genoeg miet doen of
liepen ront om onse lyf heenen sonder schaemte dit is
het derde Casteel & wert genaem[t] SCHANIDISSE den
Oversten hiet TEWOWARY Ick kreegh desen avont een
leewen rock om myn mede te decken maer hadden smorgens wel :100: luysen & aten hier veel harten vlees om &
by dit Casteel leyt veel vlacklandt & het bos vol eyken &
nooten boomen wy kreegen hier een beuer voor een elsen
yser[.]

Adi 21 ditto[:] Gongen wy smorgens heel vroech &
waeren van menige naet 4de Casteel te gaen maer doen
wy 1/2 myl gegaen hadden quaemen wy in een dorp daer
9 pr. huysen stonden ende was genaemt OSQUAGE den
Oversten was genaemt OQUOHO dat is wollef & hier
was een grooten offal daer onse gidse niet duer woude
gaen omdat het waeter overt hooft was door den grooten regen soo dat wyt wt stelden tot sanderdaechs desen
Oversten dede ons seer veel goets ende gaf ons wel te
eeten dede ons heel veel goedts want al wat inne synen
huysen was dat was voor ons ten besten hy seyde tegens
my anders niet dan dat ick syn broeder & goede vriendt
was Ja hy vertelde myn mede hoe dat hy dartich daegen
te lande gereyst hadde & daer gesien een engelsman om
de spraeck te leeren van de minquasen quaemen om de
vellen op te handelen ick vraeghden hem oft daer franse
wilden waeren by de sinnekens seyde Jae een dich ick
blyde was & docht doen wel tot myn ogemerck te coomen
ick werde hier onboden om een man te genesen die heel
sieck was[.]

Adi 22 ditto[:] Smorgens doen de son op quam syn wyt
saemen duer de offal gegaen die tot over de knyen diep
& was soo koudt dat onse kousen & schoenen soo hart
bevrosen in Corten tyt als harnessen de wilden dorsten
daer niet duer gaen maer gongen 2 en 2 met een stock
handt aen handt & doen wy 1/2 myl gegaen hadden quaemen wy in een dorp dat hier CAWAOGE daer stonden
14 huysen & een beer om te mesten wy gongen daer in
& soogen daer een pyp toback om dat onsen ouden Man
die onse gisse was seer moey was daer quaem een oudt
man by ons die ryep ons aen wellecoom wellecoom hoo
ghy moet hier te nacht blyven maer wy om onse reyse te
vervorderen gongen wech ick woude desen beer koopen
maer sy wouden hem niet misten alle desen wech staen
veel boomen gelycken haest den seuen boom hebben seer
dicke bast & dit dorp staet mede op een hoogen bergh
& doen wy noch een moeyl gegaen hadden quaemen wy
int 4de Casteel overlandt daer weynich boomen stonden
& wort genaemt TENOTOGE daer stonden :55: huysen
de sommige :100: & anderen min & meer treeden & hier
loopt de Kil verby daer voor desen van geseyt is & streckt
hier de Coers meest noorden ten westen & ten suyden ten
oosten hier tegen over de kil staen mede huysen maer wy
waeren daer niet in wandt die huysen waeren almeest vol
Cooren & de huysen in dit Casteel syn al vol Cooren &
boonen hier sagen de wilden wander toe want waeren alle
meest thuys & quaemen ons hier soo omringelen dat wy
pas door de wilden Conden gaen & nae langh passeren
quam een wilt by ons die ons mede nam nae syn huys
& daer gongen wy in dit Casteel is beset geweest met 3

reygen pallesaden maer nyue waer[en] daer geen aen
dan :6 a 7 soo dick dat het ongelovelyck was dat wilden
dat souden cunnen doen om ons te sien drongen malcanderen int vier[.]

Adi 23 ditto[:] Quam hier een man roepen en kreyten
duer enige huysen maer wy en wisten niet wat dat te
beduyden hadden & een wyltyts quam Jeronimus dela
Croix & seyde wat mach dat beduyden de wilden maecken haer reet int geweer ick vraeghde haer wat dat soude
beduyden seyden tegen myn niet wy sullen met malcander
speelen & daer waeren 4 met klophamers & een pertey
met bylen & stocken soo dat daer :20: persoonen inde wap-
enen quaemen 9 aen de eene siede & :11: aen de andere
siede daer gongen sy doen aen malcander & vochten &
smeeten enige hadden hernesse aen en storm hoeden die
sy selver maecken van dunne tienen & touwen aen malcander gevlochten dat daer geen piel noch byl door can
comen om haere seer te quetsen & nae dat sy soo een
langen tyt geschermuseert hadden soo liepen de partien
tegen malkander aen & sleepten den een den anderen
met den haiere gelyck sy haer vianden souden doen als sy
die verovert hadden & sneeden haer dan de hoofden af &
sy wilden hebben dat wy met onse pistolen mede souden
schieten maer wy gongen wech & lieten haer gaen & wy
worden desen dach genoot op :2: beeren & wy kreegen
desen dach 1/2 schepel boonen & een partey drooge aert-
bayen & liet hier ons versorregen van broot dat wy op de
reyse mede souden nemen waeronder dat enige gebacken
waeren daer nooten & Carstanien & drooge blauwebes-
sen & tsaet van sonnebloemen ingebacken was[.]

Adi 24 ditto[:] Wesende sonnendach soo sach Ick in
een huys een persoon die sieck was dese hadden by hem
ontbooden 2 van haer Meysters die hem souden cunnen genesen die sy SUNACHKOES hieten & met dat
die quaemen begonsten te singen & een groot vier aen
te legen deden het huys rontom wel dicht toe maecken
dat daer geen wint in conde coemen & doen deden ider
van haer een slangevel om haer hooft ende wossen haer
handen ende aen gesicht naemen doen den siecken persoon & leyden hem doen voor dat Groote vier naemen
een back met waeter daer sy wat medecyn in deden wossen doen een stock daer in 1/2 elle langh & staecken haer
daer mede in den keel dat men daer geen endt van sien
conden & spoogen doen den patienten op syn hooft ende
over syn heele lyf & doen hadden sy seer veel parten &
grillen met roepen en rasen inde hande te clappen gely
haer manier is met veel bewysen dan op het een & dan
op het ander dingh dat sy sweeten dat haer dat sweet van
alle canten afloopt[.]

Adi 25 ditto[:] Wesende karsdach stonden wy smorgens vroegh op & meenden naede sinnekens te gaen
maer door dien dat het stadich aen sneuden soo Conden
wy niet voort rey want niemant met ons wilde gaen om
ons goet te dragen & ick vraechden haer hoe veel Oversten dat sy waeren seyden man van 30 persoonen[.]

Adi 26 ditto[:] Smorgens werden myn 2 stucken
beeren speck gegeven om op onse reyse mede te nemen
& namen ons afscheyt met veel wtgeleydt die achter en
voor ons heenen liepen & deden anders niet dan riepen
ALLESE RONDADE dat is schiet maer wy niet wilden

schieten gongen op het laestwech wy gongen desen dach
overveel stucken vlacklandt & mede door een offal tot
over de knyen diep & meenden Int gaen meest behouden
te hebben desen dach westen noort & west dit bos daer wy
door gongen was voor aen meest eycken hout maer 3 oft
4 vren gegaen hadden bevonden wy almeest berck houdt
het sneeuden desen helen dach soo dat het seer swaer om
geen was over de bergen & nae 7 mylen gaens by gissingh
quaemen in een basten huysken int bos daer wy vier aen
stoockten & bleuen die nacht hier slaepen het sneeuden
altoos aen met harde noorde windt & heel coudt[.]

Adi 27 ditto[:] Smorgens vroegh gongen wy weder
smorgens heel moeyelick doo wel 2 1/2 sneu op sommige
plaetsen wy gongen overbergen en door kruepelbossen
wy saegen hier veel spoor van beeren & elanden maer
geen wilt hier staen Boecken bomen & nadat wy weder 7
of 8 mylen gegaen hadden vonden met de sonnen onder
ganck weder een huysken int bos met weyniech bast maer
met wat tacken van boomen daer wy weder groot vier
maeck[ten] & koocken daer sappaen het was desen nacht
soo coudt dat ick geen twee uren conde slaepen[.]

Adi 28 ditto[:] soo gongen wy weder als vooren & naedat wy :1 a 2: mylen gegaen hadden quamen wy by een
kil die soo de wilden myn seyden nae de minquasen haer
lant loopt & weder een myl gegaen hebbende quaemen wy
doen weder by een kil die nae de suyt revier toe loept so
de wilden myn seyden & hier werden veel otters & bevers
gevangen wy gongen desen dach mede over veel hooge bergen het bos vol groote boomen maer meest bercken & nae
7 a 8 myl gaens weder gedaen als boven staet heel coudt[.]

Adi 29 ditto[:] Gongen wy weder om onse reyte vorderen & naedat wy een wyl gaen hadden quaemen wy op
een seer hoogen bergh & doen wy den bergh meesten op
waeren soo viel Ick dat ick meenden dat myn de ribben
int lief anstucken waeren doch het was de meeter die van
myn houwer brack wy gongen mede door laegh lant daer
veel eycken boomen stonden & byl steelen en weder nae
7 mylen gaens vonden wy weder een hutken daer wy ons
weder leyden & maeckten daer vier & aten al ons eeten
hierop dat wy hadden wandt de wilden seyden dat wy
noch ontrent 4 mylen vandt Casteel waeren wandt de son
was meest onder doen daer noch een wilt naet Casteel
toeliep om haer te seggen dat wy souden coomen wy
souden mede gegaen hebben maer omdat wy alle grooten
honger hadden wouden ons de wilden niet mede nemen
... de coers N W[.]

Adi 30 ditto[:] Gongen wy sonder eeten naet sinnekens Casteel & doen wy een wyl gegaen hadden weesen
myn de wilden de spruyt vande revier die voort fort
Oraengien & verby het maquaesen landt daer quaem
een vrou onder wegen die ons gebraeden pompoenen
brochten om te eeten desen wech staet meest vol bercken houdt & schoon vlacklandt om te saeyen & eerdat
wy noch byt Casteel quaemen saegen daer 3 doot graeuen op de maniere als onse doot graven lanckt en hoogh
anders soo syn haer graven rondt & dese grauen waeren
rontom beset met pallisaden die sy van boomen geklooft
hadden & waeren soo sindelyck gemaeckt dat het wonder was soo waeren sy geschildert met roode & witte ende
swarte verue maer den Oversten syn graft daer was een

poort aen gemaeck & daer stondt boven op een groote
houten voogel & ront om geschildert met honden harten
& slangen & andere gedierten & doen wy 4 a 5 mylen
gegaen hadden doen baeden ons de wilden dat wy doch
souden schieten & wy schooten ons geweer los & daen
laeden wyt weder & gongen soo naet Casteel toe & saegen noort west van ons leggen een seer groot waeter &
tegen over het water geweldich hooghlandt dat inde wol-
cken lach soot scheen & nae dat ick hier te deegen nae
vraegden soo seyden myn de wilden dat in dat waeter de
fransen quaemen handelen & daer naer gongen wy vry-
moedich naet Casteel toetreden daer haer de wilden In
2 reygen deelden & lieten ons soo verby haer passeren
door haer poort de welcke wyt was daer wy door gongen
3 1/2 voet & daer stonden boven op de poort gesneeden 3
groote houten beelden als mannen waer by dat 3 bocken
waeyden die sy vande wilden haer hoofden hadden doot
geslagen & soo afgesneden & dat tot teecken van waerheyt segge overwinnege & dit tlineCasteel heeft 2 poorten
een aen de oost & een aen de west syde aen de oost poort
daer hong mede een lock maer dese poort die was 1 1/2
voot kleender Als de anderen & doe wy soo ten laesten
In den varsten syn huys gebracht worden daer vont ick
veel kennis & wy werden inden Oversten syn plaets gestelt
daer hy placht te sitten also doen ter tyt niet thuys en was
& wy waeren koudt nat & moede kregen datelyck eeten &
sy leyde goet vier aen & dit Casteel staet mede op een seer
hoogen bergh & was beset met 2 reygen pallisaden inden
ronte 767 treeden groot daer staen 66 huysen maer veel
beeter hooghen ende schoonden gemaeckt als alle andere

& waeren veel houten gevels aen de huysen die geschildert syn met veelder hande beesten sy slaepen hier meest
op verheven plaetsen meerder als enige andere wilden &
op den aftermiddach quam een vande raet by my die my
vraechden wat dat wy in syn landt deden & wat dat wy
hem brochten voor schenckasy Ick seyde hem dat wy hem
geen broohten maer dat wy hem maer eens quaemen
besoecken maer hy seyde dat wy niet en dochten omdat
wy hem geen schenkasy brocht[en] doen seyde hy hoe-
dat de fransen hier hadden by haer wesen handelen met
6 man & haer goede verering hadden gegeven wandt sy
inde vernoemde revier dit Jaer verleeden Augusti hadden
wesen handelen met 6 man wy saegen daer goede boss-
chadi bylen en franse hemden & rocken & schermessen
& desen raet parsoon dien schelden ons voor schellemen
& dat wy niet en dochten om dat wy soo weynich voor
haer vellen gauen sy seyden dat de franse 6 handt seewant voor een beuer geuen & veelder hande dingen meer
de wilden saeten hier seer dick op ons lief dat wy pas
sitten conden hadden sy ons wat willen doen wy conden
haest niet gedaen hebben maer daer was geen preykel
vandt lyf In dese revier daer hier van geseyt is daer wort
wel 6 a 7 Ja 800 sallemen geuangen Op eenen dach daer
waeren huysen van myn wel gesien 60 70 & meer salmen
algedrooght[.]

Adi:31:ditto[:] Op sondach is den Oversten van dit
Casteel tuys gecoomen & was genaemt ARENIAS met
noch een man seggende dat sy vande franse wilden quaemen & enige wilden gauen een sreeu seggende JAWE
ARENIAS dat was te seggen sy danckten hem dat hy

was gecoomen & Ick seyde tegen hem dat wy desen aen
staende nacht 3 schooten souden schieten & seyden myn
dat is wel & waeren heel wel te vreden wy vraegden haer
alle gelegentheyt van haer Casteel & van haer naemen &
hoe veer dat die van malkander laegen lagen sy met mayeys Corlen & met steenen & Jeronimus maeckten daer een
kaert van & wy rekendent alle in mylen hoe veer dat ider
plaets van malkander lach hier vertelden ons de wilden
dat op dat hooge landt mensen met hoorens woonden dat
wy by dat lack gesien hadden seyden mede dat daer veel
beuers gevangen worden maer dorsten soo verre niet gaen
om de france wilden derhalven souden sy vrede maecken
& wy schooten desen nacht 3 eerschooten ter eeren van
het Jaer onses heeren & salichmaeckers Jesu Cristo[.]

LOFT GODT BOVEN AL

INT CASTEEL ONNEYUTTEHAGE

OFT SINNEKENS   1635 Janu[ary]

Adi 1 January[:] Doen scholt ons een wilt weder voor
schellemen daer voor desen van geseyt is & was seer
quaedt soo dat Willem Tomassen soo quaedt was dat hem
de tranen langhst de oogen liepen de wilt siende dat wy
niet wel te vreden waeren vraeden ons wat dat ons let-
ten omdat wy hem soo quaedt aen saegen & saeten doen
ter tyt met haer 46 Ponen om & by ons lyf hadden sy
quadt in den sinne gehadt sy souden ons wel met handen
gegreepen hebben & sonder veel moeyten ons gedoot
hebben maer doen ick syn kraekelen langh enochh
gehoort hadde doen seyde Ick hem dat hy selver een
schellem was & begost te laggen seyde dat hy niet quaet

en was & seyde ghy moet niet quaedt wesen wy syn blyde
dat ghy hier gecomen syt & Jeronimus gaf den Oversten
2 messen 2 schaertier & enige elsen eysers & naelden die
wy mede hadden & op den avont hongen de wilden een
bandt met sewant op & enige andere geregen sewant die
den Oversten vande franse wilden mede gebracht hadde
tot teken van vreden dat de franse wilden by haer vry
moedech coomen & songen HO SCHENE JO HO HO
SCHENE I ATSIEHOENE ATSIHOENE waerop dat alle
de wilden tot 3 reysen riepen NETHO NETHO NETHO
& doen weder een anderen bandt opgehangen songen
doen KATON KATON KATON KATON doen riepen
sy weder met luyder kelen HY HY HY & nae langh raet
slaegen beslooten sy den peys voor 4 Jaeren & daer mede
gong ider nae syn hys toe[.]

Den:2:ditto[:] Quaemen de wilden by ons en seyden
dat wy noch 4 a 5 daegen mosten wachten & eerder niet
gaen dan souden sy ons goet reet maecken & met alle
nootdruft versorgen maer Ick seyde dat wy langh niet
mochten wachten maer gauen tot antwoort dat sy nae
de ONNEDAEGES gesonden hadden dat is het Kasteel
dat naest aen haer leyt maer Ick seyde dat sy ons meest
honger liet lyeden waer op sey seyden wy sullen u voor-
taen cost genoegh langen & wy worden desen dach wel 2
mael te gast genoot op beeren speck ende sallem[.]

Den 3:ditto[:] Soo quaemen daer enige oude mannen
by ons ende seyden datse onse vrienden wouden syn &
wy mosten niet vervaert wesen waer op ick haer seyde wy
syn niet vervaert & naeden middach soo vergaederden
haer hier den raet met 24 man & naedat sy langh geraet

slaecht hadden soo quam daer een oudt man by myn &
voelden of my hart oock klopten tegen syn handt & doen
riep hy dat wy niet vervaert waeren doen quaemen daer
noch 6 man van den raet & doen schoncken sy ons een
beuers rock & gauen myn dien & seyden dat is voor u
gaen dat ghy soo moede syt & weest op myn & syn voeten
& seyden daer dat is mede om dat ghy soo door de sneeu
geloopen hebt & doen wy dien opnaemen riepen sy tot 3
maelen NETHO NETHO NETHO dat is soo veel als dat
is nu wel & datelyck weder 5 losse beuers op myn voeten
neer geleyt & versochten daermede dat sy 4 handt sewant
& 4 handt lang laecken souden mogen hebben voor ider
groote beuer want wy moeten soo veer gaen met onse vellen & als wy dan al coomen soo vinden wy dickwils geen
laecken geen sewant geen bylen cetels noch niet met allen
ende hebben dan soo verlooren moeyten gedaen moeten
soo een een [sic] verren wech dan gaen & dragen ons goet
dan weermede & naedat wy soo een tyt geseten hadden
quam een out man by ons & dien vertolckden ons op een
ander spraeck & seyde wel wat ghy en seght niet of wy 4
hant sullen hebben of niet daer op ick hem seyde dat wy
geen macht daer toe hadden om haer dat te belouen maer
dat wy het den Oversten op den Manhatas seggen souden
dat onsen Commanduer was ende dat ick hem int vooriaer
alle bescheyt soude seggen & selver in haer lant coomen
doen syeden sy tegen myn WELSMACHKOO ghy moet
niet liegen & comen int voorjaer by ons & brengen ons
alle bescheyt & soo wy 4 hand krygen soo sullen wy aen
geen anderen onse vellen verhandelen & doen gauen sy
my de 5 beuers & riepen weder met luyder kelen NETHO

NETHO NETHO & doen omdat alles bondich & vast
soude wesen riepen ofte songen HA ASSIRONI ATSI-
MACHKOO KENT OYAKAYING WEE ONNEYATTE
ONAONDAGE KOYOCKWE HOO SENOTO WANY
AGWEGANNE HOO SCHENEHALATON KASTEN
KANOSONI YNDICKO dat was soo veel geseyt als dat
ick in alle dese plaetsen soude gaen want nomende alle
de Casteelen & daer soude ick vryegaen & in alle plaetsen
vry syn daer soude ick huys ende vier hebben hout & alles
wat ick vandaen hadde soude myn geworden & soo ick
naede franse woude gaen soo souden sy met myn gaen &
weder brengen daer ick wesen moste & daer op reepen
sy weder met luyder keelen 3 maelen NETHO NETHO
NETHO & myn werden weder een beuer geschoncken
& wy aeten desen dach beeren speck daer wy op te gast
genoot werden in desen Oversten syn huys werden alle
daege wel 3 a 4 reysen maeltyt gehouden & dat daer niet
gekoockt werde dat wert uyt andere huysen met groote
ketels in gebraecht want den raet quaem hier alle dagen
eeten & wy dat dan in huys is die kryegh een back vol
eeten want het is soo de manier dat yder man die hier
comt die kreycht een back vol & soo daer backen te cort
coomen soo brengen sy haer backen mede & haer lep-
els & gaen soo neder sitten neffens mal canderen daer
warden de backen dan gehaelt & dan vol gebracht want
een genode gast die en staet niet op vooren al eer dat
hy gegeten heeft dan singen sy somptyts & somptyts niet
bedancken dan de waert & gaen ider nae syn huys[.]

    Den 4 ditto[:] Quaemen hier 2 mannen by myn & sey-
den dat ick soude connen & sien hoe dat sy den duyvel

souden veriaegen maer ick seyde dat ick dat wel eer gesien
hadde maer ick most al even wel mede gaen & hier waeren
wel 12 mannen die hem veriaegen souden & om dat ick
niet alleen soude gaen soo nam ick Jeroni[mus] met myn
& doen wy daer quaemen werden het huys de vloor met
bast van bomen heel vol geleyt daer de duyvel Jaegers
over souden gaen & het waeren meest alle oude mannen & waeren alle geuervet ofte geschildert met roode
verue In haer aengesicht want als sy wat vreemts sullen wt
rechten & 3 onder desen parsonen hadden kransen om
haer hoofden daer 5 uitte kruysen op stonden dese cran-
sen waeren gemaeckt van harten haer dat sy soo weten te
tenten met wortelen van groen kruyt & in dit huys daer
werden int midden gestelt een persoon die seer sieck was
& langh hadde gaen Quynen & daer sat een ouden vrou
die hadde een schillepadt in haer handden die hol was &
daer staecken Craelen in die rammelden daer mede ende
songen daer onder hier wouden sy den duylvel vangen
& doot trappen want sy trapten alle de bast die int huys
was aen stucken dat daer geen heel bleef & waer dat sy
maer een weynich stof saegen aende meyeys daer sloegen
sy met groote verbaestheyt aen & dan blysen sy dat stof
soo nae makanderen & waeren dan soo vervaert dat yder
genoechte doen hadde met loopen al euen eens of sy den
duyvel saegen & nae langh stampen & loopen soo gong er
een naeden siecken parsoon toe & nam hem een otter wt
syn handt & sooghden siecken een tyt langh in den neck
& op den ruggen doen spoogh hy in den otter & smeet
hem op de aerde doen liep hy met grooter verbaestheyt
wech daer liepen doen weeder andere mannen naeden

otter & hadden dan sulleken apen spel dat het wonder omsien was Jae sy smeeten met vier aeten vier & smeeten soo met hiete asse & coolen dat ick het huys wt liep & ick kreegh desen dach weder een beuer[.]

Den 5 ditto[:] koft ick 4 droogt salmey & 2 stucken beeren speeck dat 9 dueym dick was & noch was hier veel dicker wy aeten desen dach boonen met beeren speck gekoockt & sonders niet gepasseert[.]

Den 6 ditto[:] sonders niet gepasseert dan lieten myn een partye steene sien daermede dat sy vier slaen als sy int bos gaen & verleegen syn dese steenen sy mede goet op vier roers[.]

Den 7 ditto[:] Creegen wy een bryef van Marten Gerriss gedateert van den laesten december met een sinck die van ons fort afquam & seyde ons dat ons volck seer moeyelyck waeren omdat wy niet tuys quaemen meenden dat wy doot geslaegen waeren wy aeten hier varse salm die geen twee daegen gevangen geweest was & ons werden 6-1/2 @ sewant wt onse notas gestoolen & kreegen die niet weder[.]

Den 8 ditto[:] Quam ARENIAS by myn & seyde myn dat hy met alle sy vellen met myn nae ons fort soude gaen met myn om te handelen & Jeronimus presenteerde hier syn rock te vercoopen maer coude niet quydt worden[.]

Den 9 ditto[:] Quaemen hier op den avont de onnedagens & waeren 6 oude parsoonen & 4 vrouwen & syn waeren seer moede gegaen brochten met haer enige beuers vellen ick gonck heenen & bedanckte haer dat sy ons quaemen versoecken sy hyeten myn wellecom & door dien dat het laet was soo gong ick weder nae ons huys[.]

Den 10 ditto[:] verbrande Jeronimus syn broeck meest
alsoo die snachs van syn lyf int vier was gevallen & den
oversten syn moeder die gaf laecken om weder te lappen
& Willem Tomassen naeydent weder[.]

Den 11 ditto[:] Smorgens te 10 uren quaemen de
wilden by myn & seyden komt int huys daer de onnedagens det raet sal sitten & sullen UE schenckaky geven
& ick ende Jeronimus die gongen heen & naemen een
pistool met ons & gongen ons nae haer syde sitten by een
out man genaemt CANASTOGEERA omtrent 55 jaeren
out & seyde tegen ons vrienden Ick ben hier gecommen
om UE te sien & met UE te spreecken waer voor wy hem
bedanckten & naedat sy een langen ty raetgehouden hadden soo quam een tolck by myn ende gaf myn 5 losse bevers voor myn gaen & dat wy haer quaemen besoecken ick
nam de beuers op & bedanckten haer daer op sy met luyder keelen 3 mael riepen NETHO & doen weder 5 losse
beuers leyden die mede op myn voeten & gauen ons die
omdat wy in syn raet huys gecommen waeren wy souden
seer veel vellen gekregen hebben tot schenckasi hadden
wy maer in syn lant gecoomen & baeden myn seer dat
ick te soomer in syn lant soude koomen & doen gaeven sy
myn noch 4 losse bevers & versochten doen mede dat sy
wat meer voor haer vellen mosten hebben & dan souden
sy ons veel vellen brengen & soo ick te soomer in haer
landt weder quam dan soude wy by ons een wilt 3 ofte 4
mede hebben om dat lack te besien & waer dat de fransen quaemen handelen met haer sloepen & doen wy onse
14 beuers op raepten doen riepen sy weder met luyder
kelen 3 mael NETHO & wy schooten 3 schooten & gauen

den Oversten 2 paer messen enige elsen & naelden & soo kregen wy ons bescheyt dat wy doen wel gaen mochten wy hadden doen noch 5 Pr. sallemen & 2 stucken beren speck dat wy soo op de rey souden eeten & wy kregen hier een party brooden & meel dat wy mede souden nemen[.]

12 ditto[:] Namen wy ons afscheyt & doen wy meenden dat alle dingen reet waeren doen wouden de wilden ons goet niet draegen 28 beuers & 5 sallemen met enige brooden alsoo sy alle genoeg hadden te draegen maer naer veel knorrens & schoone woorden soo gongen sy met goeden compaey met ons & droegen ons goet wy hadden hier veel volck die met ons liepen & riepen ALLE SARONDADE dat is schiet eens & doen wy by den Oversten syn graft quaemen daer schooten wy 3 schooten & doen verlieten sy ons & gongen van ons wegh het was omtrent 9 uren doen wy hier van daen gongen & gongen omtrent maer 5 mylen door 2-1/2 voet sneeu & was seer moeyelyck om te gaen soo dat daer noch enige wilden int bos mosten slaepen inde sneu maer wy quaemen noch in een hutteken daer wy slypen[.]

Den 13 ditto[:] Smorgens weder vroegh op de reyse & nadat wy weder 7 a 8 mylen gegaen hadden quaemen weder in een hutteken daer wy ons neder leyden om wat eeten te koocken & slaepen & ARENIAS die wees myn een plaes op een hooge bergh & sey nae 10 daegen gaens soo connen hier by een groote revier comen daer veel volck woont & daer veel koeyen en peerden syn maer mosten over de revier vaeren een heelen dach & dan noch 6 daegen gaen om daer te coomen & dit was de plaetse daer wy den 29 december verby gongen hy dede ons veel goets[.]

Den 14 ditto[:] Op sondach maeckten wy ons reede om te gaen maer den oversten woude hier van daen gaen om beren te jaegen & hier blyuen maer omdat het moey weer was soo gong ick allenich met 2 a 3 wilden & hier quaemen 2 maquaesen by ons omdat sy souden gaen & handelen eelants huyden & satteeu[.]

Den 15 ditto[:] Smorgens 2 uren voor daegen doen ick wat hadde ghegeten met de wilden doen gongh ick weder om myn reyse te vervorderen & doen het meest doncker was doen maeckten de wilden vier int bos want sy wouden niet verder gaen & ick quaem omtrent 3 uren in den avont in een hutteken daer ick den 26 december geslaepen hadde het was seer kout ick conde geen vier maecken most soo den heelen nacht gaen wandelen om de warmte te kreygen[.]

Den 16 ditto[:] Smorgens 3 uren voor den daegen met dat de maen begonde te luchten soch ich het padt dat ick ten laesten vont & quam door myn hart aengaen smorgens te 9 uren op seer groot vlack landt naedat ick een hoogen berg ouer hadde gegaen quam op een see effen pat dat door de sneeu gemaeckt was van de wilden die hier langhs gegaen hadden met veel harten vlees alsoo sy wt jaegen tuys gekoomen waeren in haer Castelen & ten 10 vren sach ich het Casteel & quam daer in ten 12 uren smiddachs & myn quaemen wel 100 menschen in haelen & wesen myn een huys daer ick in soude gaen & gaeuen myn te eeten een witten haes die sy 2 daegen verleden gevangen hadden & was gekoockt met Carstanien & kreegh daer een stuck teruwen broot by van een wilt die den 15 deses wt het fort oraengien gecoomen was & tegen den

avon[t] werden hier onder haer wel 40 vaedem sewant
omgedeelt tot testament van de wilden die vande kinder
pocken gestorven waeren in presentsy van de Oversten &
de naeste vrienden welck haer maniere soo is dat sy soo
deelen aen den oversten & de naeste vrinden & tegen den
avont gauen myn de wilden 2 beeren huyden om mede te
decken & haelden riet om onder myn te leggen & seyde
my mede hoe dat ons volck seer nae ons verlangden om
tuys te coemen[.]

Den 17 ditto[:] Quam Jeronimus & Willem Tomassen
met noch enige wilden in dit Casteel TENOTOGEHAGE
& waeren mede noch kloeck & gesont & op den avont soo
werden hier weder wel 100 vadem sewant wt gedeelt aen
den oversten & aen den vrienden vant naeste bloet[.]

Den 18 ditto[:] Gongen wy weder nae dit Casteel segge
wt dit Caste[el] om ons nae huys toe te spoeden want inde
sommige huysen daer laegen hier wel 40 a 50 harten aen
bouten gesneeden & gedroeght maer gaven ons daer
weynich van te eeten & nae 1/2 myn gaens gongen door
het dorp KAWAOGE genaemt & 1/2 myl quaemen wy in
het dorp OSQUAGO den oversten OSQUAHOO ons wel
onthaelden & wy verwachten hier den oversten AROMYAS
hier wy int Casteel TENOTOOGE gelaten hadden[.]

Den 19 ditto[:] Gongen wy smorgens weder met alder
haesten onse reyse te vorderen & doen wy 1/2 myl gegaen
hadden quaemen wy int 3de casteel SCHANADISSE
genaemt & ick sach inde sommige huysen oft daer geen
vellen waeren & ick vont daer 9 onnedages met vellen die
ick seyde dat met myn souden gaen naet 2de Casteel daer
den oversten TATUROT thuys segge TONEWEROT

thuys was die ons dadelyck wellekoom hieten & gaf ons
een seer vette harte bout die wy coockten & doen wy
saten & aeten doen cregen wy een brief van Sr. Marten
Gerrtsen met een wilt die nae ons soude soecken & was
gedateert van den 8 deses daer resolueerden wyt saemen
dat wy sitto sitto naet eerste Casteel souden gaen om op
morgen naet fort oraegien te vertrecken & quaemen nae
dat de son noch wel 3 vren hoogh was int eerste Casteel
hier lieten wy weder broot backen & packten hier onse 3
andere bevers dien wy van den oversten gekregen hadden doen wy hier eerst quaemen wy slypen hier desen
nacht & aeten hier[.]

Adi 20 ditto[:] Smorgens voordagen doen vercoft
Jeronimus syn rock voor 4 Pr. bevers aen een out man
wy gongen hier van daen een vre voor dage van daen
& doen wy hier van by gissinge 2 mylen gegaen hadden
soo wesen myn de wilden op een hooghen bergh daer
haer Casteel voor 9 Jaeren op gestaen hadden daer sy
van de Mahicans wt gedreven waeren & hadden nae dien
tyt daer niet meer willen woonen & doen wy 7 a 8 mylen
gegaen hadden bevonden wy dat de Jagers huysen ver-
brant waeren soo dat wy doen hier onder den blauwen
hemel vernachten[.]

Adi 21 ditto[:] Smorgens vroegh syn wy weder op de
reyse gegaen & naelangh gaen soo quamen wy op een ver-
keert pat dat wel het meeste begaen was maer door dien
dat de wilden de paeden beter dan wy kenden gongen
met ons weerom & nae dat wy 11 mylen gegaen hadden
quaemen weder godt loft & danck int fort oraengien den
21 Januari Anno 1635[.]

Maquase spraeck	Nederlanse spraeck
assire oft oggaha	duffels laecken
atoga	Byllen
atsochta	dissels
assere	messen
assaghe	rappie[r] lennet
attochwat	leepels
ondach	ceetels
endathatste	spyegels
tasaskarisat	schaeren
kamrewari	Elsen ysers
onekoera	sewant haer geldt
tiggeretait	cammen
catse	Bellen
Dedaia Witha	hemden ofte rocken
nonnewarory	karpoesen mussen
Eytroghe	craelen
Canagoesat	Schraepers
Caris	Cousen
achta	schoenen

Naemen van beesten soo daer vallen

aque	harten
aquesados	paerden
adiron	katten
aquidagon	Juck hoorn
senotowanne	Elant
ochquari	Beeren
sinite	bever
tawyne	otter
eyo	Minck
senadondo	vos
ochquoha	wolf
seranda	Mater

Icharofte sateeni	hondt
tali	kraen
kragequa	swaen
kahanckt	gans
schawariwane	kallekoen
schascariwanasi	Arent
tantanege	haes
onckwe	mensen
etsi	een man
coenhechti	een vrou
ochtaha	een oudt man
odasqueta	een oude vrou
sine gechtera	een vryer
exhechta	een vryster
ragina	een vader
distan	een moeder
Cian	een Kint
rocksongwa	een jongen
cannawarori	een hoer
Onentar	een swaere vrou
ragenonou	Oom
rackesie	Cousyn
anochquis	het haeyr
anonsi	het hooft
ohochta	de oren
ohonckwa	de keel
oneyatsa	de nues
owanisse	de tongh
onawy	de tanden
onenta	de nermen
osnotsa	de handen
onatassa	de vingeren
otichkera	den duyem
otsira	de naegelen
onirare	het schouder blaedt

orochquine	het rugge been
ossidau	de voeten
onera	vroulyckheyt
oeuda	Menschen dreck
onsaha	de blaes
canderes	mandelyckheyt
awasta	de klooten
casoya	een schip schuyt &
kanoo	
canossade	een huys ofte hutte
onega	waeter
oetseira	vier
oyente	hout brant hout
osconte	bast van boomen
canadera	broodt
ceheda	boonen
oneste	Mayeys
cinsie	vis
Ghekeront	sallem
oware	vlees
athesera	meel
satsori	eeten
onighira	drincken
Kattenkerreyager	grooten honger
augustuske	heel kout
oyendere	heel goedt
rockste	vriendt vrienden
jachteyendere	ten duecht niet
quane	Groot
canyewa	kleyn
wotstaha	Breet
cates	dick
satewa	alleens
sagat	dubbelt
Awaheya	doot

aghihi	sieck
sastorum	haest u wat
archoo	daetelyck
owaetsei	neu
thederri	Gisteren
Jorhani	morgen
careyago	de lucht
karackwero	de sonne
Asistock	de sterren
sintho	saeyen
deserentekar	weyden
sorsar	Aen hoogen
Cana	saet
onea	steen
Canadack ofte Cany	een sack oft mant
Canadaghi	een Casteel
oyoghi	een Kill
canaderage	een revier
Johati	een padt oft wegh
onstara	huylen
aquayesse	lachen
ohonte	Groente gras
oneggeri	riet oft stroey
Christittye	yser cooper loot
onegonsera	roode verve
cahonsye	swart
Crage	witt
ossivenda	blau
endatcondere	schilderen
Joddireyo	vechten
Aquinachoo	Quaet
Jaghacteroene	vervaert
dadeneye	speelen dubbelen
asserie	heel sterck
carente	slim of krom

odossera	speck
keye	vet
wistotcera	smeer
ostie	been
aghidawe	slaepen
sinekaty	by slaepen
Jankanque	heel moey
atsochwat	Toback
canonou	Tobackos pyp
esteronde	reegen
waghideria	sweeten
kayontochke	vlac saeylant
ononda	Bergen
Cayanoghe	eylanden
schahohadee	de over syede
caroo	hier nae toe
cadadiiene	handelen
daweyate	raet houden
agotsioha	een kraeles arm
aquayanderen	een oversten
seronquatse	een schellem
sariwacksi	een kakelaer
onewachten	een logenaer
tenon commeyon	wat wilt ghy hebben
sinachkoo	duyvel jaegen
adenocquat	medecyn salven
coenhaseren	gesont maecken
sategat	lecht hout aen vier
judicha	het brandt
catteges issewe	wanneer comt ghy weer
tosenochte	ick weet het niet
tegenhondi	int voor jaer
otteyage	den soomer
augustuske	den winter
katkaste	eeten kooken

jori	het is gaer	
dequoquoha	wt jaegen gaen	
osqucha	ick salt haelen	
seyendereii	ick kan hen wel	
kristoni asseroni	Nederlanders duytsen	
aderondacky	fransen of engelsen	
anesagghena	Mahikanders	
torsas	omde nooert	
Kanonnewage	de manhatas	
onscat	1	Een
tiggeni	2	Twee
asse	3	dree
cayere	4	vier
wisck	5	vyef
jayack	6	ses
tsadack	7	seeven
hategon	8	Acht
tyochte	9	neegen
oyere	10	Tien
tawasse	40	veertich
onscatteneyawe	100	hondert

BIBLIOGRAPHY

Abler, Thomas S., "Longhouse and Palisade: Northeastern Iroquoian Villages of the Seventeenth Century." *Ontario History* 62(1970):17–40.

Abler, Thomas S., and Elisabeth Tooker, "Seneca." In *Handbook of North American Indians*, Vol. 15, *Northeast*, edited by Bruce G. Trigger, 505–17. Washington, D.C.: Smithsonian Institution, 1978.

Adney, Edwin T., and Howard I. Chappelle, *The Bark Canoes and Skin Boats of North America*. Washington, D.C.: Smithsonian Institution, 1964.

Axtell, James, and William C. Sturtevant, "The Unkindest Cut, or Who Invented Scalping?" *William and Mary Quarterly* 37, 3(1980):451–72.

Bachman, Van Cleaf, *Peltries or Plantations: The Economic Policies of the Dutch West India Company in New Netherland, 1623–1639*. Baltimore: Johns Hopkins Press, 1969.

Beauchamp, William M., *Aboriginal Occupation of New York*. New York State Museum Bulletin 32. Albany: New York State Education Department, 1900.

———. "Indian Nations of the Great Lakes." *American Antiquarian and Oriental Journal* 17(1895):321–25.

Benson, Adolph B., rev. and ed., *Peter Kalm's Travels in North America: The English Version of 1770.* New York: Dover, 1966.

Bigger, Henry P., ed., *The Voyages of Jacques Cartier: Published from the Originals with Translations, Notes and Appendices.* Publications of the Public Archives of Canada 11. Ottawa, 1924.

Blau, Harold, Jack Campisi, and Elisabeth Tooker, "Onondaga." In *Handbook of North American Indians,* Vol. 15, *Northeast,* edited by Bruce G. Trigger, 491–99. Washington, D.C.: Smithsonian Institution, 1978.

Boxer, C. R., *The Dutch Seaborne Empire, 1600–1800.* London: Hutchinson, 1965; reprint, New York: Penguin, 1990.

Bradley, James W., *Before Albany: An Archaeology of Native-Dutch Relations in the Capital Region, 1600–1664.* New York State Museum Bulletin 509. Albany: Univ. of the State of New York, 2007.

———. *Evolution of the Onondaga Iroquois: Accommodating Change, 1500–1655.* Syracuse: Univ. of Syracuse Press, 1987.

———. "Revisiting Wampum and Other Seventeenth-Century Shell Games." Archaeology of Eastern North America 39(2011):25–51.

Brandão, José António, *"Your fyre shall burn no more": Iroquois Policy toward New France and Its Native Allies to 1701.* Lincoln: Univ. of Nebraska Press, 1997.

Brasser, T. J., "Early Indian-European Contacts." In *Handbook of North American Indians,* Vol. 15, *Northeast,* edited by Bruce G. Trigger, 78–88. Washington, D.C.: Smithsonian Institution, 1978.

———. "Mahican." In *Handbook of North American Indians,* Vol. 15, *Northeast,* edited by Bruce G. Trigger, 198–212. Washington, D.C.: Smithsonian Institution, 1978.

Bruyas, Jacques, "Radical Words of the Mohawk Language: With Their Derivatives." Shea's Library of American Linguistics 10. New York: Cramoisy Press, 1863.

Burke, Thomas E., Jr., *Mohawk Frontier: The Dutch Community of Schenectady, New York, 1661–1710*, 2nd ed. Albany: State Univ. of New York Press, 2009.

Carse, Mary, "The Mohawk Iroquois." *Archaeological Society of Connecticut Bulletin* 23(1949):3–53.

Ceci, Lynn, "The Effect of European Contact and Trade on the Settlement Patterns of Indians in Coastal New York, 1524–1665." Ph.D. dissertation, The City Univ. of New York, 1977.

———. "The Value of Wampum among the New York Iroquois: A Case Study in Artifact Analysis." *Journal of Anthropological Research* 38, 1(1982):97–107.

Clarke, T. Wood, *The Bloody Mohawk*. New York: MacMillan, 1940.

Cuoq, Jean-André, *Lexique de la langue iroquoise avec notes et appendices*. Montreal: J. Chapleau, 1882.

Day, Gordon M., and Bruce E. Trigger, "Algonquin." In *Handbook of North American Indians*, Vol. 15, *Northeast*, edited by Bruce G. Trigger, 792–97. Washington, D.C.: Smithsonian Institution, 1978.

Dennis, Matthew, *Cultivating a Landscape of Peace: Iroquois-European Encounters in Seventeenth-Century America*. Ithaca: Cornell Univ. Press, 1993.

Engelbrecht, William, *Iroquoia: The Development of a Native World*. Syracuse: Syracuse Univ. Press, 2003.

———. "The Reflection of Patterned Behavior in Iroquois Pottery Decoration." *Pennsylvania Archaeologist* 42, 3(1972):1–15.

Fenton, William N., *False Faces of the Iroquois*, Norman: Univ. of Oklahoma Press, 1987.

———. *The Great Law and the Longhouse: A Political History of the Iroquois Confederacy*. Norman: Univ. of Oklahoma Press, 1998.

———. *The Little Water Medicine Society of the Senecas*. Norman: Univ. of Oklahoma Press, 2002.

————. "The New York State Wampum Collection: The Case for the Integrity of Cultural Treasures." *Proceedings of the American Philosophical Society* 115, 6(1971):437–61.

————. "Northern Iroquoian Culture Patterns." In *Handbook of North American Indians*, Vol. 15, *Northeast*, edited by Bruce G. Trigger, 296–321. Washington, D.C.: Smithsonian Institution, 1978.

Fenton, William N., and Ernest S. Dodge, "An Elm Bark Canoe in the Peabody Museum of Salem." *American Neptune* 9, 3(1949):185–206.

Fenton, William N., and Elisabeth Tooker, "Mohawk." In *Handbook of North American Indians*, Vol. 15, *Northeast*, edited by Bruce G. Trigger, 466–80. Washington, D.C.: Smithsonian Institution, 1978.

Frey, Samuel L., *Frey Papers*. Box 9829, Folder 337. New York State Archives, Albany.

————. "Notes on Arendt van Corlear's Journal of 1634." *Oneida Historical Society Transactions* 8(1898):42–48.

Gehring, Charles T., "An Undiscovered Van Rensselaer Letter." *de Halve Maen* 54, 3(1979):13, 28.

Gehring, Charles T., trans. and ed., *New York Historical Manuscripts: Dutch. Vols. 18–19. Delaware Papers*. Baltimore: Genealogical Publishing, 1981.

Gehring, Charles T., and William A. Starna, "A Case of Fraud: The Dela Croix Letter and Map of 1634." *New York History* 66, 3(1984):249–261.

————. "Dutch and Indians in the Hudson Valley: The Early Period." *The Hudson Valley Regional Review* 9, 2(1992), 1–25.

Goddard, Ives, "Linguistic Variation in a Small Speech Community: The Personal Dialects of Moraviantown Delaware." *Anthropological Linguistics* 52, 1(2010):1–48.

———. "The Origin and Meaning of the Name: Manhattan." *New York History 91*, 4(2010):277–93.

Grassman, Thomas, *The Mohawk Indians and Their Valley*. Schenectady: Hugo, 1969.

Grayson, Donald K., "The Riverhaven No. 2 Vertebrate Fauna: Comments on Methods in Faunal Analysis and on Aspects of the Subsistence Potential of Prehistoric New York." *Man in the Northeast* 8(1974):23–40.

Greene, Nelson, ed., *History of the Mohawk Valley*. 4 vols. Chicago: S. J. Clarke, 1925.

Hart, Simon, *The Prehistory of the New Netherland Company: Amsterdam Notarial Records of the First Dutch Voyages to the Hudson*. Amsterdam: City of Amsterdam Press, 1959.

Heidenreich, Conrad E., *Huronia: A History and Geography of the Huron Indians, 1600–1650*. Toronto: McClelland and Stewart, 1971.

Herrick, James W., *Iroquois Medical Botany*. Syracuse: Syracuse Univ. Press, 1995.

Hunt, George T., *The Wars of the Iroquois*. Madison: Univ. of Wisconsin Press, 1940.

Hutchinson, Holmes, "Holmes Hutchinson Maps, vol. 9. Minden to Amsterdam" [1834]. Series 848. New York State Archives. Albany.

Israel, Jonathan I., *The Dutch Republic: Its Rise, Greatness, and Fall, 1477–1806*. New York: Oxford Univ. Press, 1995.

Jacobs, Jaap, *New Netherland: A Dutch Colony in Seventeenth-Century America*. Leiden: Brill, 2005.

Jameson, J. Franklin, ed., *Narratives of New Netherland, 1609–1664*. New York: Charles Scribners' Sons, 1909.

Jennings, Francis, *The Ambiguous Iroquois Empire: The Covenant Chain Confederation of Indian Tribes with English Colonies from*

Its Beginnings to the Lancaster Treaty of 1744. New York: W. W. Norton and Company, 1984.

————. "Susquehannock." In *Handbook of North American Indians*, Vol. 15, *Northeast*, edited by Bruce G. Trigger, 362–67. Washington, D.C.: Smithsonian Institution, 1978.

Lafitau, Father Joseph François, *Customs of the American Indians Compared with the Customs of Primitive Times*. 2 vols. Translated and edited by William N. Fenton and Elizabeth L. Moore. Toronto: The Champlain Society, 1974, 1977.

Lathers, William, and Edward J. Sheehan, "The Iroquois Occupation in the Mohawk Valley." *Van Epps-Hartley Bulletin* 2, 1(1937):5–9.

Lenig, Donald, "Of Dutchmen, Beaver Hats and Iroquois." In *Current Perspectives in Northeastern Archaeology: Essays in Honor of William A. Ritchie*, edited by Robert E. Funk and Charles F. Hayes, III, 71–84. Researches and Transactions of New York State Archaeological Association 17, No. 1. Rochester and Albany, 1977.

Loockermans to Gillis Verbrugge, Dec. 21, 1647. Stuyvesant-Rutherford Papers, 2:7a. New-York Historical Society.

Loockermans to Gillis Verbrugge, Mar. 28, 1648. Stuyvesant-Rutherford Papers, 2:7b. New-York Historical Society.

Marr, John S., and John T. Cathey, "New Hypothesis for Cause of Epidemic among Native Americans, New England, 1616–1619." *Emerging Infectious Diseases* 16, 2(2010):281–6.

McBride, Kevin A., "The Source and Mother of the Fur Trade: Native-Dutch Relations in Eastern New Netherland." In *Enduring Traditions: The Native Peoples of New England*, edited by Laurie Weinstein, 31–51. Westport: Bergin & Garvey, 1994.

Mithun, Marianne, "The Proto-Iroquoians: Cultural Reconstruction from Lexical Materials." In *Extending the Rafters: Interdisciplinary Approaches to Iroquoian Studies*, edited by

Michael K. Foster, Jack Campisi, and Marianne Mithun, 259–81. Albany: State Univ. of New York Press, 1984.

Morgan, Lewis H., *League of the Iroquois*. New York: Corinth Books, 1962.

O'Callaghan, E. B., ed., *The Documentary History of the State of New York*. Vol. 3, quarto edition. Albany: Weed, Parsons and Company, 1850.

O'Callaghan, E. B., *The Register of New Netherland; 1626 to 1674*. Albany: J. Munsell, 1865.

O'Callaghan, E. B., and Berthold Fernow, eds., *Documents Relative to the Colonial History of New York; Procured in Holland, England, and France by John R. Brodhead*. 15 vols. Albany: Weed, Parsons and Company, 1853–1887.

Parker, Arthur C., *Iroquois Uses of Maize and Other Food Plants*. New York State Museum Bulletin 144. Albany: Univ. of the State of New York, 1910.

Peña, Elizabeth S., "Wampum Production in New Netherland and Colonial New York: The Historical and Archaeological Context." Ph.D. dissertation, Boston Univ., 1990.

Pendergast, James F., "The Introduction of European Goods into the Native Community in the Sixteenth Century." In *Proceedings of the 1992 People to People Conference*, edited by Charles F. Hayes III, 7–18. Research Records 23. Rochester: Rochester Museum and Science Center, 1994.

Pratt, Peter P., *Archaeology of the Oneida Iroquois*. Occasional Publications in Northeastern Archaeology 1. George's Mill, N.H., 1976.

Reid, W. Max., *The Mohawk Valley: Its Legends and Its History*. New York: G. P. Putnam's Sons, 1901.

Richter, Daniel K., *The Ordeal of the Longhouse: The Peoples of the Iroquois League in the Era of European Colonization*. Chapel Hill: Univ. of North Carolina Press, 1992.

———. "War and Culture: The Iroquois Experience." *William and Mary Quarterly* 40, 4(1983):528–59.

Rink, Oliver A., *Holland on the Hudson: An Economic and Social History of Dutch New York*. Ithaca: Cornell Univ. Press, 1986.

Ruttenber, Edward Manning, *Footprints of the Red Men. Indian Geographical Names in the Valley of Hudson's River, the Valley of the Mohawk, and on the Delaware River: their location and the probable meaning of some of them*. New York: New York State Historical Association, 1906.

Sagard-Théodat, Gabriel, *The Long Journey to the Country of the Hurons* [1632]. Edited by George M. Strong. Translated by H. H. Langton. New York: Greenwood Press, 1968.

Shea, John D. G., ed., *A French-Onondaga Dictionary, from a Manuscript of the Seventeenth Century*. Shea's Library of American Linguistics 1. New York: Cramoisy Press, 1860.

Shimony, Annemarie Androd, *Conservatism among the Iroquois at the Six Nations Reserve*. Syracuse: Syracuse Univ. Press, 1994.

Snow, Dean R., "The Architecture of Iroquois Longhouses." *Northeast Anthropology* 53(1997):61–84.

———. "Mohawk Demography and the Effects of Exogenous Epidemics on American Indian Populations." *Journal of Anthropological Archaeology* 15(1996):160–82.

———. *Mohawk Valley Archaeology: The Sites*. The Institute for Archaeological Studies. Albany: Univ. at Albany, State Univ. of New York, 1995.

Snow, Dean R., Charles T. Gehring, and William A. Starna, eds., *In Mohawk Country: Early Narratives about a Native People*. Syracuse: Syracuse Univ. Press, 1996.

Snow, Dean R., and Kim M. Lanphear, "European Contact and Indian Depopulation in the Northeast: The Timing of the First Epidemics." *Ethnohistory* 35, 1(1988):15–33.

Snow, Dean R., and William A. Starna, "Sixteenth-Century De-population: A View from the Mohawk Valley." *American Anthropologist* 91(1989):142–149.

Starna, William A., "A Checklist of Higher Edible Plants Native to the Upper Susquehanna Valley, New York State." In *Archaeological Investigations in the Upper Susquehanna Valley, New York State*, Vol. 2, by Robert E. Funk; with contributions by Franklin J. Hesse, et al., 21–36. Buffalo: Persimmon Press, 1998.

———. *From Homeland to New Land: A History of the Mahican Indians, 1600–1830.* Lincoln: Univ. of Nebraska Press, 2013.

———. "Retrospecting the Origins of the League of the Iroquois." *Proceedings of the American Philosophical Society* 152, 3(2008):279–321.

Starna, William A., and José António Brandão, "From the Mohawk-Mahican War to the Beaver Wars: Questioning the Pattern." *Ethnohistory* 51, 4(2004):725–50.

Starna, William A., George R. Hamell, and William L. Butts, "Northern Iroquoian Horticulture and Insect Infestation: A Cause for Village Removal." *Ethnohistory* 31, 3(1987):197–207.

Starna, William A., and Ralph Watkins, "Northern Iroquoian Slavery." *Ethnohistory* 38, 1(1991):34–57.

Thwaites, Reuben Gold, ed., *The Jesuit Relations and Allied Documents: Travels and Explorations of the Jesuit Missionaries in New France, 1610–1791.* 73 vols. 1896–1901. Reprint, New York: Pageant, 1959.

Tooker, Elisabeth, *An Ethnography of the Huron Indians.* Bureau of American Ethnology Bulletin 190. Washington, D.C.: Bureau of American Ethnology, 1964.

———. *The Iroquois Ceremonial of Midwinter.* Syracuse: Syracuse Univ. Press, 1970.

————. "The League of the Iroquois: Its History, Politics, and Ritual." In *Handbook of North American Indians*, Vol. 15, *Northeast*, edited by Bruce G. Trigger, 418–41. Washington, D.C.: Smithsonian Institution, 1978.

Trelease, Allen W., *Indian Affairs in Colonial New York: The Seventeenth Century*. Ithaca: Cornell Univ. Press, 1960.

Trigger, Bruce G., *The Children of Aataentsic, A History of the Huron People to 1660*. 2 vols. Montreal: McGill-Queen's Univ. Press, 1976.

————. "Early Iroquoian Contacts with Europeans." In *Handbook of North American Indians*, Vol. 15, *Northeast*, edited by Bruce G. Trigger, 344–56. Washington, D.C.: Smithsonian Institution, 1978.

Van der Donck, Adriaen, *A Description of New Netherland, by Adriaen van der Donck*. Edited by Charles T. Gehring and William A. Starna. Translated by Diederik Willem Goedhuys. Lincoln: Univ. of Nebraska Press, 2008.

Van Laer, A. J. F., "Arent van Curler and His Historic Letter to the Patroon." *Dutch Settlers Society Yearbook* 3(1927–1928):11–29. Albany.

Van Laer, A. J. F., trans. and annot., *New York Historical Manuscripts: Dutch. Vol. 1. Register of the Provincial Secretary, 1638–1642*. Baltimore: Genealogical Publishing, 1974.

————. trans. and annot., *New York Historical Manuscripts: Dutch. Vol. 2. Register of the Provincial Secretary, 1642–1647*. Baltimore: Genealogical Publishing, 1974.

————. trans. and annot., *New York Historical Manuscripts: Dutch. Vol. 3. Register of the Provincial Secretary, 1648–1660*. Baltimore: Genealogical Publishing, 1974.

————. trans. and annot., *New York Historical Manuscripts: Dutch. Vol. 4. Council Minutes, 1638–1649*. Baltimore: Genealogical Publishing, 1974.

Van Laer, A. J. F., trans. and ed., *Documents Relating to New Netherland 1624–1626 in the Henry E. Huntington Library*. San Marino: Henry E. Huntington Library and Art Gallery, 1924.

———. trans. and ed., *Minutes of the Court of Rensselaerswyck, 1648–1652*. Albany: The Univ. of the State of New York, 1922.

———. trans. and ed., *Van Rensselaer Bowier Manuscripts: Being the Letters of Kiliaen van Rensselaer, 1630–1643, and Other Documents Relating to the Colony of Rensselaerswyck*. Albany: Univ. of the State of New York, 1908.

Van Loon, L. G., "Letter from Jeronimus de la Croix to the Commissary at Fort Orange and a Hitherto Unknown Map Relating to Surgeon Van den Bogaert's Journey Into the Mohawk Country, 1634–1635." *Dutch Settlers Society Yearbook* 15(1939–1940):1–9. Albany.

Venema, Janny, *Beverwijck: A Dutch Village on the American Frontier, 1652–1664*. Albany: State Univ. of New York Press, 2003.

———. *Kiliaen van Rensselaer (1586–1643): Designing a New World*. Albany: State Univ. of New York Press, 2011.

Waterman, Kees-Jan, ed. and trans., *"To Do Justice to Him & Myself": Evert Wendell's Account Book of the Fur Trade with Indians in Albany, New York, 1695–1726*. Philadelphia: American Philosophical Society, 2008.

Waugh, Frederick W., *Iroquois Food and Food Preparation*. Geological Survey Memoir 36, Anthropological Series 12. Ottawa: Government Printing Bureau, 1916.

White, Marian E., "Erie." In *Handbook of North American Indians*, Vol. 15, *Northeast*, edited by Bruce G. Trigger, 412–17. Washington, D.C.: Smithsonian Institution, 1978.

———. "Neutral and Wenro." In *Handbook of North American Indians*, Vol. 15, *Northeast*, edited by Bruce G. Trigger, 407–11. Washington, D.C.: Smithsonian Institution, 1978.

Wilson, General James Grant, "Arent Van Curler and His Journal of 1634–25." *American Historical Association Annual Report for 1895*, Pp. 81–101.

———. "Corlear and His Journal of 1634." *The Independent* 47(Oct. 3, 1895):1–4.

Wright, Benjamin, "An Examination of the Country for a Canal from Rome to Waterford on the North Side of the Mohawk River" [1811]. Manuscript Collection. Erie Canal Museum Library. Syracuse.

Zeisberger, David, *Zeisberger's Indian Dictionary: English, German, Iroquois—The Onondaga and Algonquin—The Delaware.* Cambridge, Mass.: John Wilson and Son, 1887.